ENTERING HIS PRESENCE

ENTERING HIS PRESENCE

Experiencing the joy of true worship

DON McMINN

Bridge Publishing, Inc.
South Plainfield, New Jersey 07080

Scripture references are taken from the New American Standard Bible (NAS), unless otherwise indicated.

Entering His Presence
© 1986 by Bridge Publishing, Inc.
Printed in the United States of America
ISBN 0-88270-608-X
Library of Congress catalog number: 86-70743
Bridge Publishing, Inc.
2500 Hamilton Blvd.
South Plainfield, NJ 07080

"To Mary, Lauren, and Sarah—
my praise-life companions."

Table of Contents

Foreword ix
Preface xi
1　The Chief End of Man 1
2　Worship—The "Opus Dei" 7
3　The Delocalization of Worship 17
4　Offerings in Righteousness 24
5　Christ Praising Through Us 29
6　The Childlikeness of Praise 35
7　We Never Did It That Way Before 41
8　Seven Times a Day, I Will Praise Thee 47
9　Lord, I Believe! Therefore I Praise Thee 53
10　Overcoming Through Praise 57
11　Judah—The Tribe of Praise 63
12　Pouring Out Offerings to the Lord 69
13　Thy Praise Shall Continually Be in My Mouth ... 75
14　He Made Us to Praise Him 81
15　On Earth as It Is in Heaven 87
16　Dancing Unto the Lord 95
17　Lifting Holy Hands Unto the Lord 101
18　Singing—The Christian's Right and Privilege .. 107
19　Praise Him in Song 111
20　Performance Standards for God's Musicians ... 119

21	The Song of Fools	127
22	The Lord Inhabits the Praises of His People	133
23	Praise—The Offensive Weapon	139
24	Psalms—The Heart of Biblical Praise	149
25	The Fruit of Our Lips	157
26	The Vocabulary of Praise	169
27	Rocks, Be Silent!	179
28	Lessons From the Tabernacle	185
29	Praise the Name of the Lord	193
30	Vain Worship	199
31	Evangelism and Praise	207
32	Restful Worship	213
33	The Highest Praise	217
34	Leading People in Worship	223
35	The Tabernacle of David	231
36	In the Year King Uzziah Died	237
37	Upon Leaving His Presence	243
38	Becoming Uninhibited	249
	Selected Bibliography	257

Foreword

My deep conviction is that one of the marks of God upon church history during the last two decades of the twentieth century will be that of the reinstatement of praise in the Body of Christ.

Don McMinn's work on the subject of praise will be greatly used to implement this reinstatement. When one is speaking to a matter about which he does not feel deeply, many words seem to be the order of the day. This does not describe my feelings regarding this work. Thus I am not forced to be unduly wordy about my recommendations.

This work is completely biblical, totally relevant, intensely practical, thoroughly personal, and positively readable.

The reader will find the writing style conducive to any kind of reading. It can be read quickly with great benefit but will be as equally rewarding to the reader who loves to curl up with a good book on a lonely evening to spend hours reading slowly.

It is filled with ideas for implementing personal praise. I have taken note of many of them and plan to use them in my own spiritual journey in discovering worship.

I find great joy in introducing you to what I feel will be a grand experience of worship and praise.

                    Jack Taylor
                    President,
                    Dimensions for Christian Living

Preface

I recently heard of a church in the Southwest that called a special business meeting to vote on one issue: whether or not they were going to praise the Lord. Regardless of what the outcome of the vote was, the fact that such an issue was placed on the agenda probably placed that church in spiritual default. Praise is not an option; it is an imperative! If we do not practice praise, we walk in disobedience. The issue of praise is not up for discussion or vote: the Lord *will* be praised. Jesus made this perfectly clear when He told a "praiseless" group of Pharisees that if the disciples' shouts were silenced, the very stones they were standing on would cry out in praise (Luke 19:40).

God is restoring the ministry of praise and worship in His body. Churches all across America are discovering the same joy that the Israelites experienced when the ark of the covenant was placed on Mount Zion. They offered free and uninhibited praise day and night. And just as the Israelites responded in praise to the presence of God in the ark, God's people are lifting up shouts of praise as God tabernacles among us today. Traditions are crumbling

(Isa. 29:13), the fear of man is losing its grip (John 12:42-43), and God's people are confessing as sin their being ashamed of Jesus (Mark 8:38). They are learning to confess aloud the excellencies of Him who brought us out of darkness and into His marvelous light (1 Pet. 2:9). We are seeing the bride making herself ready! We are learning the vocabulary of heaven to avoid culture shock when we arrive! God's people are discovering that it is a good thing to give praise unto the Lord (Ps. 92:1), that there's nothing wrong with it (Ps. 33:1), and that it's even scriptural (it's in the Bible)!

The divine pursuit mentioned in John chapter four has always intrigued me: the Father seeks those who will worship Him in spirit and in truth. It is expedient for us to seek the Lord and we are encouraged to do so many times in Scripture, but it seems unusual that He would seek us. I find it amazing that God would seek our worship. But just as a father desires the love of his children (we are His children) and a husband needs and desires the love of his wife (we are His bride), so the Lord desires our worship. To embrace the contrary would put in question the entire motivation of creation. God created us for His pleasure (Rev. 4:11), without in any way jeopardizing His deity. If the knowledge of God's motivation in creating man will not convince us of His desire for fellowship and mutual love, certainly the act of redemption will. God paid the costliest ransom in the universe so that we might once again be worshipers of God. If it was not the dearest thing to His heart, surely the price of His Son would have been too much.

It not only amazes me that God seeks worshipers, but I find it startling to realize that He finds very few. Ostensibly the greatness of God as expressed in nature should be sufficient prompting for a worldwide deluge of true worship.

Preface

But alas, worshipers of God are rare. That which was intended to be our "modus operandi" has become our point of greatest temptation and travail. Every day we are faced with the issue: will we worship the Lord and Him only?

What happens when we are found by God? This is the obvious implication of John four. If the Father seeks those who will worship Him in spirit and in truth, and we begin to worship Him in spirit and in truth, a divine encounter occurs. We are found by God! God begins to reap the benefit of His creative endeavors, we begin to fulfill our eternal mission, and all of creation rejoices at such satisfacation.

I want to be a worshiper of God. I want to worship in a manner pleasing to Him. I desire to learn all I can about the subject so that, to the degree knowledge is of benefit, I will be helped. It is from this posture that I share with you the beginnings of my journey into the rich and rewarding ministry of praise and worship.

1
The Chief End of Man

God made us to be worshipers. The ultimate purpose of God in creating man was that we might spend eternity in awesome adoration of His Person. The philosophical question posed to us by the Presbyterians, "What is the chief end of man?" is answered by the catechism, "To glorify God and to enjoy Him forever."

When God created Adam, He did not do so with the thought of preparing one who would serve Him; He already had a host of angels who would serve Him and do so perfectly. Nor was His fashioning of man for the purpose of expanding His resources or adding to His available source of counsel, for God is all in all, complete in himself, and His wisdom needs no counsel.

In the creation process, God formed the light and the darkness and called them good. They, in some small manner, reflected the glory of God. Next He created the firmament, the dry land, and the seas. With each new element, the glory of God was magnified with greater intensity. The earth sprouted forth vegetation and fruit-bearing trees which reflected the life of God. The sun, moon, and stars were created and the seasons began their cycle, all giving evidence of the faithfulness of God. The creation process began to accelerate with the fashioning of fish, fowl, and living creatures that walked on the earth. These creatures possessed not only a body, but a soul, and could function using their minds, wills, and emotions.

Yet God was not satisfied. Though what He had created reflected His glory and gave tribute to His magnificence, it could not respond to Him in praise and worship. God was like a beautiful sound which could not be heard, a lovely flower which no one could see, a beautiful statue gone unnoticed. Man was created in the image of God that he might have the capacity to know God, and, in so knowing, would adore Him. The most godlike thing in the universe is the spirit of man, and it was made that way so we might know and worship God. When God created man, He looked upon His creation and said, "It is very good."

God made us to be worshipers; but in Genesis three, the Bible tells us that man forfeited his privilege to commune with and admire the Holy Trinity. God designed us to be volitional devotees and we chose wrongly. In so choosing, we lost sight of the purpose for which we were created and simultaneously precipitated the redemptive process which would make possible the reinstatement of God's purpose. A.W. Tozer describes what happened in the garden:

> God gave to man a harp and said, "Here above all the creatures that I have made and created I have given you the largest harp. I put more strings on your instrument and I have given you a wider range than I have given to any other creature. You can worship Me in a manner that

The Chief End of Man

no other creature can." And when he sinned man took that instrument and threw it down in the mud and there it has lain for centuries, rusted, broken, unstrung; and man, instead of playing a harp like the angels and seeking to worship God in all of his activities, is ego-centered and turns in on himself and sulks and swears and laughs and sings, but it's all without joy and without worship.*

God sent His only Son, Jesus, into the world for one reason: to redeem man so that he could once again take his place, along with the holy angels, before the throne of God. Some think that Christ came to save us from bad habits, or to keep us from going to hell, or to prepare for us an eternal "resting place" in heaven. These are all true: salvation does give us power over sin; it does keep us out of a devil's hell; and it will ensure for us a heavenly estate; but that is not the ultimate purpose of the incarnate Christ dying on a Roman cross. He died that we might once again be worshipers of God. When Christ, by His death, rent in twain the veil of the temple, mankind could once again enter into the Holy of Holies. The Holy of Holies is not a place of service, nor one where we go to do good deeds or works. It is a place of worship, it is where we encounter God in all His glory, and where we worship Him in the beauty of holiness.

We do new converts a grave injustice. When one is born again, we immediately make a worker out of him. We involve him in all sorts of fine Christian service and he spends hours "serving the Lord." We first need to train

---

* A.W. Tozer, *Worship The Missing Jewel*, p. 11.

these new converts in the art of worship, after which they can become workers. An even greater tragedy exists in the case of many saints who have been saved for years but have seldom, if ever, entered into true worship. I am afraid these saints may feel a little awkward their first few moments in heaven.

For years we have been taught that the great commission is to be found in Matthew 28:19-20, but according to the testimony of Jesus it is found in Matthew 22:36-38. A lawyer had asked Jesus a question, wanting to test Him: "Teacher, which is the great commandment in the law?" Without pausing to sort out among several close alternatives, the Lord answered, "You shall love the Lord your God with all your heart, and with all your soul, and with all your mind. This is the great and first commandment" (RSV). Notice Jesus did not say you shall *serve* the Lord your God—we must place our worship above our serving.

It is like when I give my daughter a list of things to do and specifically designate the order in which they are to be done. She is to do this item first, this item second, and so on. She may say, "Daddy, I do not want to do number one; instead I will do twice the amount of number two." Regardless of how much she does of the lesser priorities and the zeal with which she may do them, my heart is not satisfied. We must likewise be cognizant of and obedient to the supreme priority which God has given us. Jesus said to Peter three times, "If you love me, feed my sheep." Indirect love is not sufficient. Loving the Lord by loving others is not sufficient; we must love Him directly. Having established our love for Him, we can then "feed the sheep."

The highest compliment God ever gave man was to create him in such a way as to desire his admiration. Just as

The Chief End of Man

I desire fellowship from my children, God needs our fellowship. Just as I am incomplete without my wife, Christ is incomplete without His bride, the Church. It was God who made the first move in creating us, and the second move in redeeming us. He made us as much like himself as He could. We are fashioned in His image in order that we might worship Him.

We all have individual goals and objectives which we pursue throughout our lifetime. My wife and I sit down every December and pray over our plans and goals for the coming year. As Christians, our plans are only successful to the degree that they correspond with God's will for our life. A planning session for a Christian is basically a time of seeking the mind of the Lord for our future. Why not get in on God's ultimate purpose for man? Why not plan on participating this year in the "ultimate aim" of mankind? Be a worshiper of God!

The anonymous author of this seventeenth-century Spanish poem was right on target in his theology and life direction. The final stanza in itself faultlessly answers the age-old question "What is the chief end of man?"

> My God, I love Thee;
>   Not because I hope for heaven thereby.
> Nor yet for fear that loving not
>   I might forever die;
> But for that Thou didst all mankind
>   Upon the cross embrace;
> For us didst bear the nails and spear,
>   And manifold disgrace,
> And griefs and torments numberless,
>   And sweat of agony;

E'en death itself; and all for man
    Who was Thine enemy.

Then why, most loving Jesus Christ,
    Should I not love Thee well,
Nor for the sake of winning heaven,
    Nor any fear of hell;

Not with the hope of gaining aught,
    Not seeking a reward;
But as Thyself hast loved me,
    O ever-loving Lord!

E'en so I love Thee, and will love,
    And in Thy praise will sing,
Solely because Thou art my God
    And my eternal King. Amen.

2
Worship—The "Opus Dei"

My wife and I are in the process of rearing two daughters. Like all Christian parents, we have a desire to raise them in the fear and admonition of the Lord. There are so many truths to teach, so many character traits to develop; it is always a challenge to be complete in our instruction and their training. Though we try to maintain a thoroughness in our teaching, sometimes I cannot help but prioritize in my mind the teachings we consider to be important. I have even asked myself, "If I could only impart to my daughters one truth, what would it be? If they learn nothing else from their father, what is the one thing I must give them?" I could teach them to pray, for that is certainly a priority in the Christian life. I could convince them of the need to be faithful to a local Bible-believing church, because there they would receive instruction and encouragement. Another good first choice would be to encourage them to learn the ways of love, for the Bible says that it is greater than even faith and hope. It would also be important to teach them the importance of living a sanctified life, for they must learn how to deal with sin and how to appropriate the holiness of Christ. Or how about the need for obedience, both to God and to the authorities God places over them?

I have settled the issue in my mind: If I could teach my children only one thing, I would teach them to be worshipers of God, for when one truly worships God, all else is well!

If my children truly worship God, they will by nature attend church, they will seek the experience of prayer, they will always find sin repulsive, they will consider obedience a privilege, and their norm will be love. It is true that when we sincerely worship God, all else is well. Whenever we commune with God Almighty and enjoy the glory of His presence, our lives are put into proper spiritual condition.

What is this thing called worship? Who has experienced it? What does it feel like? How do I become a worshiper of God? The answers to these questions have always seemed elusive, but they need not be. God made us to be worshipers; therefore it must be within the grasp of all saints, and it is certainly in consonance with the will and desire of the Lord.

Some definitions may help to further our understanding.

The Hebrew word for worship is *shaha.* It means to "bow low" or to "prostrate" oneself. Worship involves our bowing low before the Lord, not only physically, but in our hearts. It involves a reverential fear of God. When Abraham's servant was awed by the Lord's power in leading him to find Isaac's wife, he bowed low and worshiped the Lord. (See Gen. 24:48.)

The Greek word for worship is *proskyneo,* which literally means to "kiss the hand of one who is revered" or to "do obeisance to another." It is used 59 times in the New Testament.

Worship—The "Opus Dei"

The English word *worship* comes from the Anglo-Saxon *weorthscipe* which denotes one who is worthy of honor and reverence. When we worship God, we are declaring to Him His worth; we are confessing to Him that He is worthy. In Revelation 4, the twenty-four elders worshiped the Lord by confessing that He is worthy to receive glory, honor, and power.

It is always encouraging to know that, for those who seek the Lord, He will be found (Jer. 29:13). If we seek God in worship, we will have a worship experience. If we hunger and thirst after righteousness, we will be filled (Matt. 5:6). I have discovered through the years that it is not those who "study" worship that enjoy His presence, but rather those who seek Him. There is a sense in which worship defies definition and analysis. We can look back at a worship experience and study the circumstances that prompted worship; we can enumerate the elements that were involved; we can describe how we felt afterwards; but to use these to establish a pattern or formula for worship is futile.

Worship encounters seem to be spontaneous, fresh, and, usually, initiated by God. For Moses it came while he was in the desert: "Then He said, 'Do not come near here . . . for the place on which you are standing is holy ground'. . . . And then Moses hid his face" (Exod. 3:5, 6 NAS). Another time Moses was on Mount Sinai when God met him: "And Moses made haste to bow his head low toward the earth and worship" (Exod. 34:8 NAS). Solomon and the priest met God at the dedication of a building, "and when the song was raised . . . the house of the Lord was filled with a cloud, so that the priests could not stand to minister because of the cloud; for the glory of the Lord filled the house of God" (2 Chron. 5:13, 14 RSV). The Lord came to the early church while they were together in an upper room: "they were all with one accord in one place. And suddenly there a sound came from heaven . . . and they were filled with the Holy Spirit" (Acts 2:1-4 KJV).

The scope of worship seems to be both wide and narrow, depending on perspective. In many respects, prayer is worship, giving is worship, witnessing is worship, Bible study is worship; in general, any act of obedience initiated and led by the Spirit of God is worship. Some even feel that their daily work, if done in a manner pleasing to God, is worship. On the other hand, many consider worship one of those mystical events in which the supernatural is more than evident. I am inclined to acknowledge both, though not willing to settle for one without the other. There is a degree to which my works can express my worship of God, but there must come a point in which God expresses himself to me in a personal, supernatural way. True worship always involves receiving from God; it is God pouring His life into us.

Praise and worship are wonderfully related and it is often difficult to determine when praise ceases and worship begins. However, the ministry of praise and the experience of worship are uniquely different. They share many common concerns but they are not the same.

Praise is acknowledgment; worship is relational.

Praise is unidirectional—we praise God; He does not praise us. Praise is our acknowledgment of His power, authority, wisdom and worthiness. Praise does not require a response from the one who is being praised; it is one-way communication. Worship, however, is relational: it is not only our confession of God, but His response to us.

Worship—The "Opus Dei"

Worship is a love relationship, one in which both parties give of themselves.

Praise usually precedes worship.

The Psalmist has written, "Enter His gates with thanksgiving, and His courts with praise" (Ps. 100:4 NAS). The children of Israel went to the tabernacle to meet God, and there He revealed himself to them. As we begin our entrance into God's presence, we engage in praise. Praise, then, is a means of coming into His presence; worship is what we do when we get there.

There is great danger in stopping at praise and not entering worship, though I am afraid that this is often the case. Obviously there is nothing wrong with praise, but praise is a means to an end and not the end itself. If praise does not lead us to God, the cycle is short-circuited. God is the end! God's presence is where we want to be and His voice is what we want to hear. It would have been of no value for the priests to "enter His gates with thanksgiving" if they did not eventually arrive at the Holy of Holies, the place where they met God.

In one sense, praise is fun; it is enjoyable. We clap, we sing, we have a good time. I do not want to imply that worship is not enjoyable, but at times it can be very exacting. In a time of worship God may convict us of sin; in His presence we may be called to Nineveh. Regardless of what takes place, we must make it to worship!

In Exodus 33:16, Moses gave the mark of distinction for God's people: "For how then can it be known that I have found favor in Thy sight, I and Thy people? Is it not by Thy going with us, so that we, I and Thy people, may be distinguished from all the other people who are upon the face of the earth?"

God is with us—this is to be the distinguishing factor in our lives. In the environment of praise, the Lord distills upon His people, and worship is the divine touch which transforms our lives. If God is to go with us, we must provide for Him a constant coronation of praise and an ever present commitment to worship Him.

Praise is situational; worship is focused on the eternal.

Praise is usually prompted by circumstances. We experience the goodness of the Lord, so we praise Him; or we encounter trying and difficult situations and we are prompted to praise as an expression of our faith. Praise is often initiated and centered around the immediate, that which our senses can perceive. Worship, however, is focused on the eternal. During worship we are usually elevated to such spiritual heights that we see not the incarnate Christ but the glorified Christ, seated at the right hand of the Father. We do not notice other saints, only the eternal God. The circumstances of this world are not a part of our worship experience; during worship they become out of focus and very insignificant. The issue in worship is not "what He has done" but "who He is." Even His magnificent works become secondary to His splendid attributes and character. God is the subject of our worship. One identification of God is "the worship object of the universe."

In praise we give to Him; in worship we give to Him and receive from Him. In my church we often sing this chorus of praise, "We bring the sacrifice of praise, into the house of the Lord, And we offer up to you the sacrifice of praise."

Worship—The "Opus Dei"

But we also sing this chorus of worship, "Spirit of the Living God, fall fresh on me. Break me, melt me, mold me, fill me, Spirit of the Living God fall fresh on me."

It seems that in praise we exclusively give to Him. There are certainly many benefits we receive from engaging in the act of praise but these seem to be "built into the system" rather than spontaneously given by the Father. However, in the act of worship we not only give to the Father, but He gives to each as He wills. Often we do not even know what we have received, for many times we do not know what we need. Sometimes, during a worship encounter He simply pours into our spirit a more abundant manifestation of His Spirit. We may leave His presence with many fears cast out because a perfect love has flooded our beings (1 John 4:18). We may leave delivered from condemnation because we have entered into Christ more fully (Rom. 8:1).

Perhaps the most beautiful and illustrative verse on worship in the entire Bible is Revelation 3:20: "Behold I stand at the door and knock; if anyone hears My voice and opens the door, I will come in to him, and will dine with him, and he with Me." For years we have missed the meaning of this verse because we have misinterpreted to whom the Lord is speaking. I have shared the gospel message with scores of people and used this verse as part of my closing. In essence, I say to the lost man, "if you will simply open your heart and invite Jesus to come in, He will save you." I am sure this approach meets with God's approval, because the basic concept is reinforced throughout the Scriptures. However, we know that Revelation was written for the church—not for the unsaved. Revelation 3:20 offers *us* a beautiful invitation from the Father to come and worship

Him. And notice the reciprocal approach which is advocated: we will dine with Him, and He will dine with us! This is the dynamic of worship: we give ourselves to Him, but He also gives himself to us!

In the sixth chapter of Isaiah, the prophet shared with us a wonderful worship experience (vs. 1-8), an account which thrills our hearts and gives us insight into what it means to worship God. Isaiah had this encounter in the year King Uzziah died. Though the King of Judah was dead, the God of Judah was alive and reigning. Isaiah saw the Lord Jesus (John 12:41) and He was high and lifted up and the train of His robe filled the temple. The sight which he saw was one of magnificent grandeur. The Lord's throne was "lofty and exalted," indeed, the throne of the universe. Those attending the throne were holy angels called seraphim, who are innumerable and whose pleasure is to offer praise to God (Dan. 7:10). Isaiah heard them call out, one to another, "Holy, Holy, Holy, is the Lord of hosts, the whole earth is full of His glory." The praise was so intense that the door sockets trembled at the sound and the house was filled with smoke.

Isaiah's first concern was that he did not belong in this place because he was a man of unclean lips. In prostration, he confessed to God his impurity. God is always true to His Word. "If we confess our sins, He is faithful and righteous to forgive us our sins and to cleanse us from all unrighteousness" (1 John 1:9). No sooner did Isaiah confess his unclean lips than an angel touched his mouth with a burning coal and took away his iniquity.

The end result of Isaiah's worship encounter was twofold: Isaiah confessed a renewed consecration to the will of God, and he received revelation from God. He received new life and direction. Regardless of the circumstances surrounding a worship experience, the end result will always be a deeper commitment to God's will, and a renewed insight into His desire for our lives.

In Revelation 11:1, John was commanded to "Rise and measure the temple of God, and the altar, and those who worship in it." God is concerned with our worship. It is not something He considers to be optional in our daily life and practice. Could it be that someday God will measure our praise life? If so, I do not want to be found lacking; if anything, when I get to heaven, I hope to fit right in with what is going on. I want to be measured, and found complete!

3
The Delocalization of Worship

There is a group of people who are very dear to God. According to the Bible God the Father seeks them. Their main characteristic is that they *know how to worship God:* "But an hour is coming, and now is, when the true worshipers shall worship the Father in spirit and truth: for such people the Father seeks to be His worshipers" (John 4:23).

As it was in the days of Christ, so it is today: there are few true worshipers. There are many who work for God, many who perform Christian services, many who go through disciplined ritual, but few who worship God as He has specified and as He requires.

John, in chapter four, related an interesting encounter Jesus had with a Samaritan woman at Jacob's well. The woman had a longing inside her which she did not know how to satisfy. She had sought contentment through relationships with men (having been married five times and then living in adultery with a sixth man), but she was not satisfied—she needed God! Within every person there is a longing for God, a desire to know Him. Most people misinterpret this yearning and attempt to fill the void with varied fleshly activities. Some turn to a hobby, others to a relationship, others to alcohol or narcotics. Paul sensed this false fulfillment when he said, "Do not get drunk with wine, for that is dissipation, but be filled with the Spirit" (Eph. 5:18). When God designed man, He built in a need for God that nothing else will satisfy!

The conversation between the Lord and this Samaritan woman soon moved to the topic of worship. Her basic misunderstanding of worship centered around placing too much importance on its location. There was a time in the life of God's people (it was an issue even to those who worshiped false gods) when worship relied heavily upon location and upon an edifice where the worship would take place. By stating that her fathers worshiped God on the mountain, the woman was challenging the Jewish belief that Jerusalem was the ideal place to worship. Jesus replied that there could come a time when men would worship neither on the mountain nor in Jerusalem, but that they would find the presence of God in their spirits and would worship Him there. In essence, Jesus delocalized worship!

We are also guilty of this false assocation of worship to place. We have been so programmed to think that the worship service takes place on Sunday morning, and that it occurs in the sanctuary that we have missed the real essence of worship. Christ has taught us that the worship of His Spirit must take place in our spirits. Though a Christian be all alone, and even secluded in a meaningless location, he still has all he needs to worship God. He not only has all he needs, he has all he can get! A beautifully esthetic structure may enhance our emotional involvement or provide a point of orientation, but it will not ensure worship,

The Delocalization of Worship

and in some instances may hinder it. God is spirit, as opposed to flesh; therefore He is unlimited and nonlocalized. He can, and will, abide and commune within every regenerated spirit that seeks the revelation of God.

Man's spirit is the one place where he can meet God. We are tripartite in nature: we each have a body, soul, and spirit (1 Thess. 5:23).

The body, which is the temple of the Holy Spirit, provides awareness of the physical world through the five senses.

The soul involves consciousness of self and others; it consists of three parts: the will or volition, which is the instrument of decision making (Job 6:7, 7:15); the mind or intellect, which is the instrument of thought, reason and memory; and the emotions, which consist of feelings, affections and desires (1 Sam. 18:1; Deut. 14:26; Ps. 84:2, 86:4).

The spirit, which involves consciousness of God and the supernatural world, consists of conscience and discernment of right and wrong (2 Cor. 2:13); intuition, which perceives knowledge without use of the soul or the five senses (John 11:33, 13:21; Mark 2:8; Acts 20:22); and the capacity for communion, worship, and communication with God (John 4:23; Rom. 8:16; 1 Cor. 14:15).

Adam was created with all three areas: "God formed man of dust from the ground [body], and breathed into his nostrils the breath of life [spirit]; and man became a living being [soul]" (Gen. 2:7). All men have resident within them these three areas. However, before we are born again, our spirit is present but inactive in its relationship to God. It takes the redeeming work of Christ to enlighten our spirit and make it responsive to God. Prior to our salvation the spirit is dormant. This is why it is impossible for a non-Christian to comprehend the things of God, to converse with God, or to worship Him. Only after our spirit is awakened from latency can we fellowship with His Spirit. There can be no communciation between different natures (1 Cor. 2:10-16).

We worship God with our spirit and in our spirit—this is true worship. Untrue worship would be to worship Him with our body (ritual, physical movements, sacraments) when our spirit is void of participation. Even to worship with our mind, will, and emotions would be futile if they were not in consonance with the direction of our spirit. Let me quickly add that there is nothing wrong with incorporating the body and the soul in the worship experience. They must, however, be subordinate to the activity of the spirit. We must also defend ourselves against the thinking that to become physically or emotionally involved in worship is wrong. It is not! God wants the whole man to worship Him! It is all a matter of preeminence and origin. God works from the inside out (spirit, soul, body), and so all spiritual activity must originate in the spirit. Furthermore, He desires that the spirit of man, controlled by the Spirit of God, be ruler over the other two parts.

Judson Cornwall said, "The greatest cause of failure in worship is our attempt to perform it before we arrive in God's presence." Before we worship Him, we must go where He is. The Spirit of God resides not in the soul or body of man, but in his spirit, and it is there we must turn if we hope to engage in worship.

Therefore, Jesus' discourse with the Samaritan woman was intended to teach her the real essence of worship, her lack of it, and her need for a Savior to secure it. The Samaritans had a form of worship on Mount Gerizim, but

The Delocalization of Worship

they denied the One to be worshiped. Even the ceremonial observances of the Mosaic institution would soon have been inadequate since the Lord would move His residence from the temple made with hands to the temple of our spirits. Though it is not specifically stated, the closing verses of this episode imply that the woman at the well did indeed believe unto salvation; that she received the everlasting water, and, no doubt, learned how to worship Jesus.

Some may think worship in spirit is lacking in some aspects, or that we cannot perceive Christ as clearly as if He were with us in the flesh. Quite the opposite is true. We see Jesus more accurately and more clearly in the spirit than in the flesh. Compare the gospel of John and the Revelation of John. Though John caught a glimpse of who Jesus was when he walked with Him, when he was "in the spirit on the Lord's day" he saw the indescribable One in such glory that he "fell at His feet as a dead man" (Rev. 1:10, 17). The revelation given him in his spirit was the most personal and exacting he had ever experienced.

Our worship of God will be no greater than our knowledge of God. To the extent we know God, to that degree we can worship Him. In this respect, every believer has a different capacity to worship. Some are so backslidden that they have not received any fresh revelation from God in years. They have not seen or acknowledged God's powerful work in their lives. It is no wonder they cannot worship God—they do not know Him, they have not spent time with Him. On the other hand, how sweet are the hours of worship for one who has made it his life-long quest to know Him.

The Father still seeks true worshipers—has His searching

eye found you? Why not get off by yourself right now and in the quietness of your own spirit, meet God and worship Him?

4
Offerings in Righteousness

Righteousness and praise are inextricably related. It is impossible for true worship to exist where there is sin and unrighteousness. To the contrary, Jesus is always in the midst of holiness, and where Jesus is made manifest, praise will soon follow.

This is a principle the New Testament church must learn if its worship is to be genuine and effective. There are numerous spiritual activities we can become involved in after confession and cleansing, but there are none which can precede. Even if we begin our worship service with thanksgiving and praise, we must first claim the blood of Jesus for our lives before we get to the inner court. When the Levitical priest entered the outer court of the tabernacle, the first article of furniture he encountered was the brazen altar. It was there that he would sacrifice an animal as an act of atonement. He dared not proceed through the rest of the ceremonies until the blood had been spilt. Communion with God was impossible until righteousness had been established.

Because we are all believer-priests, we can and must seek

personal cleansing. Christ's work on the cross provided cleansing for all saints who ask for it with a repentant heart (1 John 1:9). Cleansing is a difficult thing to attempt corporately. Only in the case of corporate sin is corporate confession of any value.

If this principle is true for all saints, it is particularly pertinent to those who are in a position of leadership in the worship service. Of the priest, God said, "[I] will sit as a refiner and purifier of silver, and [I] will purify the sons of Levi and refine them like gold and silver, till they present right offerings to the Lord" (Mal. 3:3 RSV). It is an awesome thing to stand before God; but to lead people to God in worship, and to minister to the Lord himself, is beyond the realm of the awesome. It is a task which should be fearfully approached. "Who may ascend into the hill of the Lord? And who may stand in His holy place? He who has clean hands and a pure heart, who has not lifted up his soul to falsehood, and has not sworn deceitfully. He shall receive a blessing from the Lord" (Ps. 24:3-5).

The psalmist tells us that the Lord inhabits the praises of His people. This is why our praise must be administered in righteousness. The same admonition God gave to the children of Israel applies to our "camp" today. "Since the Lord your God walks in the midst of your camp to deliver you and to defeat your enemies before you, therefore your camp must be holy; and He must not see anything indecent among you lest He turn away from you" (Deut. 23:14). God is uncompromising in regard to holiness. He will not tolerate the presence of sin and will simply withdraw His presence if sin continues to exist.

We must never think that praise will in any way appease God or act as a substitute for confession. If we walk into the

Offerings in Righteousness

---

sanctuary with sin in our life and proceed to enter into a time of praise, at the end of that time we will still have sin in our life. David said, "thou dost not delight in sacrifice, otherwise I would give it; Thou art not pleased with burnt offering. The sacrifices of God are a broken spirit" (Ps. 51:16-17). We make a mockery of ourselves when we attempt to approach God in praise when there is known sin in our lives. The only way to God is through the cleansing power of the blood. Only after we have received cleansing can we begin to truly praise and worship Him. This was Isaiah's first concern when he saw the Lord "high and lifted up." He exclaimed, "Woe is me, for I am ruined! Because I am a man of unclean lips . . . for my eyes have seen the King, the Lord of hosts" (Isa. 6:5). It was only after the seraphim purified his tongue with a burning coal that he was able to be at peace in the presence of the Lord. It is interesting to note that David, the praise-leader of Israel, praised much and sinned much. Right in the midst of Israel's songbook is the penitent Psalm (Ps. 51). David found that his praise and his sin were incompatible, but he had a successful praise-life because he had remorse for his sin and freely confessed to the Lord.

One of the best times for the church to enter into praise is following the ordinance of the Lord's Supper. If it has been administered properly, the serving of the ordinance is preceded by a time of soul-searching and confession. We have been correctly taught to reverence the sharing of the elements (probably because of an emphasis on 1 Corinthians 11:28-30). At the conclusion of the supper, most of the saints are right with God, Christ is pleased because of our obedience, and a joyful time of praise can be shared by all.

Entering His Presence

It is interesting to note that the unrighteous man cannot, and will not, enjoy praise. The unsaved will feel very much out of place in a praise service. Even the Christian who is in the flesh will have very little patience with an emphasis on praise and worship. But a Christian living in the power and control of the Holy Spirit will always enjoy a time of magnifying the name of Jesus.

At times, however, we will approach a time of praise with all known sins confessed only to experience an unusual phenomenon. Although to the best of our knowledge we have placed every sin under the blood of Christ, in the midst of our time of praise a past sin which has gone unconfessed is brought to the forefront of our consciousness. Perhaps a sin of years gone by is brought to mind with the same clarity as if it had happened the day before.

I used to think this was Satan attempting to thwart my time with God; the evil one was bringing to mind former failures. Then God opened up my understanding of Proverbs 27:21, "As the fining pot for silver, and the furnace for gold; so is a man to his praise" (KJV). As the furnace is heated, the dross from the alloy begins to rise to the surface, separating itself from the pure metal. With each new level of heat intensity, more and more dross rises to the surface to be removed by the master artisan. So it is in a time of praise. As our spirits are ignited by the fire of God, sin that has eluded consciousness is brought to the surface in order that we may confess it, and God may remove it. Deeper levels of praise will result in more and more sin revealed. If we deal with it properly, our spirits will become increasingly pure before God.

There are many references in the Bible that speak to the

Offerings in Righteousness

interdependence of praise and righteousness. Let them speak to our hearts:

> For as the earth brings forth its sprouts, and as a garden causes the things sown in it to spring up, so the Lord God will cause righteousness and praise to spring up before all the nations (Isa. 61:11).
>
> Thy testimonies are fully confirmed; holiness befits Thy house (Ps. 93:5).
>
> The sacrifice of the wicked is an abomination to the Lord, but the prayer of the upright is His delight (Prov. 15:8).
>
> Ascribe to the Lord the glory due to His name; worship the Lord in holy array (Ps. 29:2).
>
> As for me, I shall behold Thy face in righteousness (Ps. 17:15).
>
> My eyes shall be upon the faithful of the land, that they may dwell with me; he who walks in a blameless way is the one who will minister to me. He who practices deceit shall not dwell within my house; he who speaks falsehood shall not maintain his position before me (Ps. 101:6, 7).

5
Christ In Us—
Praising Through Us

That Christ is in us, working through us, is a wonderful truth. In fact, the only way we can live the Christian life is to let Christ live His life through us. The Father said, "This is my beloved Son in whom I am well pleased." If we ever hope to please the Father, it will be because He sees Jesus, not us. All spiritual thought and activity must originate from the throne, be received in our spirits, and be executed by the Holy Spirit who is resident within us. As such, we are simply channels through which God can operate.

When we preach, we receive the truth of God's Word in our spirits, and ask the Spirit of God to preach through us. When we witness, it is His Spirit that precedes us and works through us in the sharing experience. When we minister in song, it must be Christ ministering through us if we are to be effective. The principle is no less true in regard to praise and worship. If our praise is to be of any consequence, it must be the resident Christ praising through us.

There are two verses in Hebrews which accentuate this truth. The first is Hebrews 13:15:

> Through Him then, let us continually offer up a sacrifice of praise to God, that is, the fruit of lips that give thanks to His name.

In verses 9-14 of this chapter, the writer makes it clear that those who persist in observing the Old Testament ceremonial laws and sacrifices will have no share of the blessings of the New Covenant. As we read through the book of Leviticus our spirits are weighted down with all of the detail and burdensome requirements of the law. It makes us want to exclaim with the hymn-writer, "Free from the law! O happy condition!" As believer-priests, we are to continue to offer sacrifices, but they are not to be expiatory sacrifices for there is no need of them; Christ has offered once for all the perfect sacrifice. We are to offer sacrifices of *praise* because our hearts are full of love and adoration for Christ.

Note that it is "through Him" that we can make the transfer from animal sacrifices to the sacrifices of praise. Because of the meritorious atonement and intercession of Christ, we no longer live under the encumbrance of the law. We are free to worship Him in spirit and in truth. In essence, Jesus made praise possible; without Him we would know nothing of godly matters or concerns. Without His redeeming work, we would have no basis for communion.

Not only is praise made possible through the work of Christ, but Hebrews 2:12 indicates that it is actually Christ in us who is praising the Father through us:

> I will proclaim Thy Name to My brethren, in the midst of the congregation I will sing Thy praise.

Christ In Us—Praising Through Us

This passage is a quote from Psalm 22:22. The entire psalm is clearly a prophetic utterance of Christ and His earthly ministry. It begins with the very works spoken by Christ on the cross, "My God, My God, why hast Thou forsaken Me?" and concludes with the exaltation of Christ and the salvation and joy of His people. Its reference to Christ is confirmed by the writer of Hebrews, for he uses this verse to illustrate the brotherly relationship Christ has with those who believe.

Matthew Henry gives keen insight into the verse:

1. Christ should have a church in the world, a company of volunteers freely willing to follow Him.
2. These should not only be brethren to one another, but to Christ Himself.
3. He would declare His Father's name to them, that is, His nature and attributes, His mind and will.
4. Christ would sing praise to His Father in the church.*

Isn't it wonderful to know that Jesus sings! And that He sings through us! (Incidentally, the Father [Zeph. 3:17] and the Holy Spirit [Eph. 5:19] also sing.) It is a marvelous thought that this Old Testament prophecy is being fulfilled every time the local church gathers to worship and praise. Next time you sing "Holy, Holy, Holy" in church recall the truth of this verse, and see it does not heighten your experience knowing that it is Jesus in you singing to the Father:

---

* Matthew Henry Commentary (Sovereign Grace Pub.: 1972), Vol. I, p. 185.

Holy, holy, holy, all the saints adore Thee,
Casting down their golden crowns around the glassy sea;
Cherubim and seraphim falling down before Thee,
Who wert, and art, and evermore shall be.

—Heber

Obviously, there is no one who knows the Father as well as the Son. They have spent eternity-past together, will spend eternity-future together, and always experience uninterrupted, perfect communion. Indeed, they are One. The inference derived from this fact is simple: since no one knows the Father as well as the Son, no one can praise the Father as well as the Son! I can appreciate and praise my wife more fully and intelligently than others can because I know her best. In like manner, no one is more eminently qualified to praise the Father than His only Son, Jesus. Just as the Spirit prays for us when we do not know how to pray, the same Spirit praises through us in ways and to degrees not attainable on our own.

I recall a minister who once shared his view that most Christians go through three stages: they think the Christian life is easy to live; they think the Christian life is difficult to live; they realize the Christian life is impossible to live.

The third stage represents the position God wants us to be in—a sense of total helplessness apart from Him. We must realize that every godly thought or action is impossible to perform in our own flesh, but that Christ in us lives His life through us. Only then can godliness come forth from these mortal bodies. If our praise is to be of merit and to be effective, we must approach God in righteousness and Christ must be in us, praising through us. What a joy to release ourselves to this truth! Next time you want to praise

Christ In Us—Praising Through Us

God, let Jesus take over. His praise will lift your spirit to new heights of glory!

This is my wonderful story, Christ to my heart has come;
Jesus, the King of Glory, finds in my heart a home.

Now in His bosom residing, this my glad song shall be;
I am in Christ abiding, and Christ abides in me.
—Simpson

6
The Childlikeness of Praise

During our Lord's triumphal entry into Jerusalem, the multitudes were going before Him saying: "Hosanna to the Son of David! Blessed is He who comes in the name of the Lord! Hosanna in the highest!" (Matt. 21:9).

The streets were filled with praise as palm branches were placed in His path. Perhaps for the first time in His earthly ministry, Jesus was receiving the public praise He so rightfully deserved. Many were even bold enough to suggest that He was the Messiah, the long-awaited Son of David. His entrance, riding on that donkey, caused such a stir that the entire city was asking, "Who is this?" There is quite a lesson to be learned right there. When we praise Jesus in a grand fashion, all those around us will ask, "Who is this man you are praising?" What a stage will be set for us to share with them how God can invade their lives through the person of Jesus Christ! One of the best ways to spread the gospel is to publicly praise the Savior.

Jesus rode into Jerusalem and went directly to the Temple. There He rebuked and cast out those who were buying and selling, and He overturned the table of the moneychangers. Jesus then began to heal the blind and the lame who were brought to Him. An intriguing statement is made in Matthew 21:15. The Bible records that the scribes and Pharisees, who were cautiously observing Jesus, became indignant when, in the midst of the Temple, a group of people began once again to praise the Lord, crying aloud, "Hosanna to the Son of David!" Interestingly enough, that group of people consisted exclusively of children. What happened to the "multitudes going before Him and those who followed after Him" (v. 9) when He made His triumphal entry? Why were the adults not praising Him in the Temple as they had in the streets? The answer lies in an important characteristic of praise: Praise must be childlike in character. Not childish, but childlike. Jesus was pleased with the children. His comment was, "Have you not read, 'Out of the mouth of infants and nursing babes Thou hast prepared praise for Thyself?' " (v. 16). He enjoyed what the children were doing, protected them from verbal abuse by the scribes and Pharisees, and stated in essence, "You have a lot to learn from these children."

What is it about children that makes them prime candidates to lead in the praises of Jehovah? What characteristics do they have that we as adults seem to lose somewhere along the way? I would like to suggest a few: children are uninhibited in their actions; they are hard to intimidate; they possess great faith; and they are teachable and open to instruction.

I am teaching my children to praise the Lord. (It *is* something that must be taught and learned!) It is always refreshing to see their lack of inhibition. Every time they raise their arms to take their shirt off over their head, they say, "Hallelujah!" Right in the middle of a department store

The Childlikeness of Praise

one will say, "Glory to God!" Last winter we often gathered with the neighborhood kids out in the snow and began talking about Jesus and singing praise songs. They were totally uninhibited about confessing Jesus in the presence of their friends! Children seem to have an absence of self-consciousness. They so easily lose themselves in their surroundings. They are so truthful and so trusting with anyone and everyone. Somewhere between childhood and adult life, we become reserved, shy, perhaps even embarrasssed about verbally praising God—particularly in non-Christian company. We fear being labeled fools for Christ (though Paul boasted of it in 1 Cor. 4:10), when in fact most people are either fools for Christ or fools for the devil. Children do not care what others around them are doing and do not care what others think, but we are always so concerned about what is proper. To the Christian, that which is proper is what God wants us to do! It may have seemed improper for Christ to spit on the ground, take the mud, put it on a blind man's eyes and tell him to go wash; but it was proper because it was exactly what the Father dictated. If our praise is to be pleasing to God we must rid ourselves of man-induced inhibition. We must stop looking around to see what everyone else is doing and start doing what He commands. We should be less concerned about what man thinks of us than we are about what God thinks of us and our actions.

When Jesus was riding on that donkey, multitudes were praising Him in the streets, but only the children continued to praise Him in the Temple. I believe the adults ceased to praise because they were intimidated by the scribes and Pharisees. Intimidation is spawned in our hearts by a lack of faith (Mark 4:40). It is obviously not of the Lord (2 Tim. 1:7).

We are intimidated when we focus our minds on the power of man rather than the power of God. The children in this story were not at all intimidated by those pious religious leaders, who were mere men to the children (and to God)! To the children, temple praise was no less in order than street praise. Not so with the adults, who no doubt feared these men, what they were thinking and what they might say or do. The adults probably predicted the scribes' and Pharisees' response to this public outburst of praise and intentionally refrained from joining in. What an opportunity they forefeited.

This is a good lesson for us to learn from the children. We should so focus our eyes on Jesus that we are unconcerned about the opinions and actions of those who may not understand, or who sit in judgment on the working of God in His people.

Throughout the Bible, children are complimented for their sincere, effective faith. In Matthew 18, Jesus even said that if we are not converted and do not become like children, we will not enter the kingdom of heaven. It is so much easier for a child to receive the things of the Lord than for an adult: there is no intellectual argument, no hardened will to deal with, no pride to hurdle; just a simple faith. I suppose naivete is considered a liability in most instances, but in regard to our obedience to the Lord, perhaps it is an asset. Peter was rather naive to think that he could walk on water, but his naivete projected him into the realm of the supernatural, even if only for a short walk! Our faith should be like a child's faith—not asking questions or trying to figure out the situation, just obeying.

A child's mind is so pliable, so teachable. Curiosity combines with receptiveness to produce an ideal teaching

The Childlikeness of Praise

environment. The world has not had an opportunity to influence the young mind with humanism and other vain philosophies which attempt to throw doubt on the teachings of God's Word. It is important that we teach our children, at an early age, to praise and worship the Lord. They are never too young to enter into communion with God and what they learn as a child they will incorporate into their adult life. I have often said, if I had only one thing to teach my children, I would teach them to worship God. When we truly worship, all else is well.

We must become and remain teachable in regard to our acceptance and practice of spiritual truth. Fresh winds of the Spirit continue to illuminate areas of God's Word and this illumination must meet with our full and unreserved acceptance.

> Permit the children to come to Me, and stop hindering them, for the kingdom of God belongs to such as these. Truly I say to you, whoever does not receive the kingdom of God like a child shall not enter it at all. (Luke 18:16-17)

7
We Never Did It That Way Before

Several years ago there was a phrase in popular use which, though intended to be humorous, contained a very pointed indictment against the mindset of present-day churches. It read: "The Seven Last Words of the Church: 'We never did it that way before.' "

Indeed, it seems as if our churches easily fall into a complacent redundancy which often becomes a rut (a rut is sometimes defined as a grave with the ends kicked out). In no other area is this routine more deadly than in the area of worship and praise.

Many of our churches use the same order of worship they used fifteen years ago. If the Spirit of God is still freshly anointing it, fine; but when we begin to consider the form of worship sacred and ignore its function, we slowly end up in spiritual rigormortis. It is highly possible for a church to conduct three "worship services" a week and never worship the living God.

The children of Israel were guilty of the same complacency:

> Then they set out from Mount Hor by the way of the Red Sea, to go around the land of Edom; and the people became impatient because of the journey. And the people spoke against God and Moses, "Why have you brought us up out of Egypt to die in the wilderness? For there is no food and no water, and we loathe this miserable food."
>
> And the Lord sent fiery serpents among the people and they bit the people, so that many people of Israel died. So the people came to Moses, and said, "We have sinned, because we have spoken against the Lord and you; intercede with the Lord, that He may remove the serpents from us." And Moses interceded for the people. Then the Lord said to Moses, "Make a fiery serpent, and set it on a standard; and it shall come about, that everyone who is bitten, when he looks at it, he shall live." And Moses made a bronze serpent, and set it on a standard; and it came about, that if a serpent bit any man, when he looked to the bronze serpent, he lived (Num. 21:4-9).

They had unjustly complained about God's provision for them, and God in return, by withdrawing His protective hand, allowed fiery serpents to smite the people—serpents which the wilderness had been infested with all along (Deut. 8:15). Because of their repentance and supplication, the Lord provided a unique way to deliver the children of Israel from death. It was His way of showing himself strong on their behalf.

Moses was instructed to make a fiery serpent, which he constructed out of bronze, and to place it on a high pole so that those who looked to it might be healed. This was a foreshadowing of Calvary, as Christ explained in John 3:14, 15: "And as Moses lifted up the serpent in the wilderness, even so must the Son of Man be lifted up, that whoever believes may in Him have eternal life."

What began as a glorious manifestation of God's power became a stumbling block for years to come. We read in 2 Kings 18:1 that "Hezekiah . . . became king . . . and he did right in the sight of the Lord . . . he removed the high places, and broke down the sacred pillars, and cut down the Asherah. He also broke in pieces the bronze serpent that Moses had made, for until those days the sons of Israel burned incense to it; and it was called Nehushtan [a piece of bronze]." For over three hundred years they worshiped that piece of bronze; they made it an idol. They continued to worship the form after the power of God had long departed!

We say, "How could they?", and yet we are guilty of the same misunderstanding. Instead of following the cloud by day and the fire by night, we stay in one place and pray that the cloud and fire will stay upon us. The Holy Spirit is free to move as He desires through any number of forms or people, and He is on His own timetable. In our own worship, both private and corporate, we have experienced the power of God through a song, a message, a particular order of worship, or even at a particular time of day. But God is not obligated to work in those same ways.

Not only are we reluctant to break away from old forms which have lost their power, but we are often unwilling to accept new means of expression. The singing of choruses is a good example of this. In this generation, God's Spirit is moving mightily through these simple Scriptures and praise choruses. Yet many resist their use. A greater indictment is our disinclination toward using certain means to praise Him which are encouraged in the Bible. How long has it been since you or your church participated in the following:

> Praising Him with shouting
> (Ps. 35:27, 47:1, 95:1)
> Bowing down before Him
> (Ps. 95:6; Eph. 3:14; Phil. 2:10-11).
> Praising Him by clapping our hands
> (Ps. 47:1, 98:8).
> Lifting holy hands before the Lord
> (Ps. 63:4, 134:2, 141:2).
> Praising Him with shouting and a joyful noise
> (Ps. 66:1-2, 95:1; Isa. 12:6).
> Praising Him with music
> (Ps. 47:6, 57:8, 150).

Some of the most meaningful corporate worship services I have ever experienced were ones marked by spontaneity; they did not follow a "normal" planned order. I once had a pastor give the altar call after the special music because God's Spirit had settled in during the singing. In one service we had the preaching first, followed by the singing, which helped to solidify and confirm the spoken Word. Some of the best solos I have ever heard were sung by people I called up from the audience; they had not planned on singing but were ready to give an account of the joy within them. Impromptu personal testimonies have always added a freshness to worship services.

We Never Did It That Way Before

This is not to say that one cannot find the mind of God a week in advance regarding what should transpire in a service; but I do firmly believe that the one leading worship must be tuned into the voice of the Spirit, and he must be in a position of submission if the Spirit directs last-minute change. It does not take a walk with God to work through an order of worship; it does take a walk with God to hear His voice and obey.

Orderliness is an attribute of God and should certainly be evident every time we meet together. But there must also be spontaneity—a fresh anticipation and acceptance of how God wants to minister to us and through us. As master of ceremonies, He has the authority to direct the worship time as He pleases. The Holy Spirit is grieved by our ignoring His leading: "This people draw near with their words and honor Me with their lip service, but they remove their hearts far from Me, and their reverence for Me consists of tradition learned by rote" (Isa. 29:13).

Through the years of my ministry, I have had folks come up to me voicing complaints about the worship service. Sometimes the comment is, "I do not like to sing all those choruses" or "Why do we sing those old stately hymns" or "I think our services are too loud; I prefer a quiet, reverent service." What we have here is a gross misunderstanding of the worship service. Who are we attempting to please in the service—ourselves or God? It is not a matter of what we like, but what pleases God. The question to ask is not "What songs do I enjoy?" but rather "What songs does the Father enjoy listening to?" Just a cursory glance into Revelation will convince us that worship around the Throne of the Universe involves some unusual sights and sounds; but obviously they are pleasing to the One who sits upon the throne. We merely limit our worship experience when we refuse to go beyond the boundary formed by our preferences and by what we feel comfortable in doing.

It is important that our attitude toward worship be one of openness and freedom. The Lord may ask us to do something we have never done before. He may require us to change direction at the last moment, or to cancel a previously scheduled activity in the worship experience. Whatever He asks, we will do. We will approach each opportunity of worship with a fresh anticipation of the Holy Spirit's leading and His anointing of our meeting together.

> Set my spirit free,
> That I may worship Thee.
> Set my spirit free,
> That I might praise Thy Name.
> Let all bondage go
> And let deliverance flow.
> Set my spirit free to worship Thee.

8
Seven Times a Day, I Will Praise Thee

Praise should be a daily occurrence in the life of God's people. We never run short of matter for which to praise Him. If our praise were based on our feelings, then our rejoicing would be sporadic; if it were dependent upon favorable circumstances, our own interpretation of situations would dictate our praise life. To the contrary, our praise has its foundation and prompting in the character, attributes, and perfect ways of Him who never changes. Our praise should be unceasing because the object of our praise is unalterable. "Seven times a day I praise Thee, Because of Thy righteous ordinances" (Ps. 119:164).

Our praise should not only become a day-by-day occurence but a moment-by-moment experience. It eventually should become a life style, a permanent "bend" in our personage, a type of outlook we have on life. Scripture tells us:

Rejoice in the Lord always (Phil. 4:4).
Rejoice always (1 Thess. 5:16).
His praise shall continually be in my mouth (Ps. 34:1).

> My praise is continually of Thee (Ps. 71:6).
> My tongue also will utter Thy righteousness all day long (Ps. 71:24).
>
> From the rising of the sun to the going down of the same, the Lord's Name is to be praised (Ps. 113:3).

I once heard a sermon entitled, "Practicing the Presence of Jesus." There is no better way to stay in the presence of Jesus than to continually have a heart full of praise and a song on our lips. I have known believers who had such a walk. You could speak to them any time of the day, morning or evening, any day of the year, and they would have the praise of God on their lips and a smile on their face. When in their presence, you sensed another, holy presence. These folks are always a joy to be around; they invariably have an optimistic outlook and an encouraging word to share. Our lives should have such a nature. We should have the "mark" of praise on our day-to-day existence. Such a daily walk as that will totally revolutionize our actions, reactions, and mental attitude; in general, it will change our life!

In Psalm 119:164, the psalmist gave us a good formula for developing a consistent praise-life. David made it a habit of offering praise to the Lord seven times a day. I believe there were seven specific times which David put on his appointment book, at which point he stopped what he was doing, and for a designated period of time offered praise to the Lord. They were not necessarily lengthy periods of time but they were consistent and directional. I can just imagine David, the mighty King of Israel, around mid-morning, consulting with his military commanders regarding an upcoming battle with the enemy. Rather abruptly he stops the proceedings and says, "Gentlemen, it's time to praise

Seven Times a Day, I Will Praise Thee

the Lord! Let's take a few moments here to worship Jehovah." After a time of singing and testifying, they resume their duties. Again, around mid-afternoon, during a discussion with his political advisors, David interrupts the conversation, and in the midst of all those present, he begins to praise the Lord. We often think we are too busy with our daily activities to honor the Lord. Such thinking is nothing but erroneous conceit. If a man of David's stature could take the time, so can we.

What a magnificent way to ensure a great day. If one figures sixteen waking hours per day, the psalmist suggests that we praise Him about every two and a half hours. What an ingenious plan to maintain a godly perspective throughout the day. How could we harbor frustration, anger, or bitterness if we praised every two hours. What a defense against temptation and sin—how could an evil presence bear such consistent praise? What a testimony it would be to those around us if they witnessed our devotion and love for the Lord so many times every day.

In attempting to be consistent and disciplined about something you want to do every day, it always helps to identify certain activities which are fixed—those activities which, if not performed, will soon bear ill-fated results. Once these are identified, other functions can be tagged on and will immediately become consistent. I can think of five of these activities which are a part of most people's schedule: waking up, eating breakfast, lunch and dinner, and going to sleep. Based upon these events, I suggest a praise schedule similar to this: 1. praise the Lord as soon as you wake up in the morning, even before you get out of bed; 2. offer praise before you eat breakfast, or during the meal; 3. mid-morning, around 10:00 A.M., pause to praise Him; 4. praise

Him before or during lunch; 5. mid-afternoon, around 3:00 P.M., schedule a few minutes; 6. around the dinner table speak of the goodness of the Lord; and finally, 7. before you go to sleep at night, offer to God the sacrifice of praise. I have often challenged people to try this schedule for one full week. Most folks can do just about anything for one week if they really put their mind to it. Without exception the week becomes a glorious experience. Sometimes lives are changed during the course of their "praise marathon."

One might ask, "What do I do during these seven recesses?" The options are many, and are only restricted by your imagination and openness to the creative leadership of the Lord. Activities might include the following: read a Psalm out loud; memorize and sing several verses from a great old hymn; sing a chorus of praise; express gratitude to the Lord for His faithfulness, mercy, and grace; verbally ascribe the glory due His name; witness to a lost person; testify to someone as to how the Lord was strong or faithful in your life; make up an original praise song using your own words or one of the Psalms; tell the Lord how much you love Him.

There must come a time in our life when we see praise as a necessary part of our Christian experience and there must come a time when we devote ourselves to the task of learning to praise. It comes easier for some than others but it is something that we must conscientiously try to develop in a life style and walk with the Lord. Claus Westermann, a German scholar, learned to praise while he was interned in a Nazi prison camp during World War II. Though he only had a New Testament and the book of Psalms, he emerged from the years of imprisonment as one who had the mantle of God on his shoulder. In his book,

The Praise of God in the Psalms, Westermann commented on a particular group of Christians who became overcomers of the cruel circumstances they were forced to live in:

> Whenever one in his enforced separation praised God in song, or speech, or silence, he became conscious of himself not as an individual, but as a member of the congregation. When in hunger and cold, between interrogations, or as one sentenced to death, he was privileged to praise God . . . this praise out of the depths has become an argument that speaks louder than the arguments we have been accustomed to bring forth for "Christendom."*

Whether it is in distress or in prosperity, we must learn to praise Him. Our lives would drastically change if we became praise-minded people.

I challenge you to maintain the above-mentioned praise schedule for one week and just see if your life will not take on new meaning and a new perspective.

---

* Claus Westermann, *Praise and Lament in the Psalms,* p. 10.

9
Lord I Believe! Therefore I Praise Thee

The impetus of praise is belief in God. The more we believe in God, the more we will praise Him. Those who do not believe in God have no reason to praise Him. To the extent that we acknowledge His sovereign work in our lives, to that degree will our praise ascend.

Psalm 106 gives a poetic history of the children of Israel during their exodus from Egypt. In verse twelve we read, "then they believed His words; they sang His praise." Their lips were silent until they saw the mighty hand of God in deliverance; then, having belief in their hearts, their lips were vibrant with praise. How much better it would have been had their praise preceded God's actions (John 20:29). A little later in their pilgrimage the Bible says, "they did not believe in His Word, but grumbled in their tents" (Ps. 106:24-25). What a clear word of instruction for us! When we truly believe God and trust in His Word, our hearts are full of praise; but when our hearts are full of unbelief, we begin to murmur and grumble. "For the mouth speaks out of that which fills the heart" (Matt. 12:34).

At the basis of all praise there is the element of faith. When our faith wavers, so does our praise. When our faith is strengthened, our praise increases. We are often burdened down with a problem or a trying circumstance. We go to the Lord in prayer and to His Word, seeking an answer from the Throne. When the answer comes, faith is kindled in our hearts and it becomes the basis for our praise. I remember once praying for a four-week-old baby with multiple physical complications at birth. Praise was present from the beginning of the ordeal because the parents and I had faith that God was in control. However, I soon received a Rhema from God's Word that the boy was to live (John 1:4). The parents received the word as from the Lord, and there was great rejoicing! "Faith comes by hearing, and hearing by the Word of Christ" (Rom. 10:17). Faith comes by hearing and praise comes by faith. Faith always precedes praise and praise is perhaps the best means of expressing the faith that is within us.

The timing of praise is always important. Many people praise only when the victory has been realized, only when the strong hand of God is evident. God wants us to praise Him when it seems there is no way out, when the tunnel is still dark and victory seems elusive, if not improbable. This is the faith/praise that pleases God. In 2 Chronicles 20:20, Jehoshaphat and the Kingdom of Judah were surrounded by the enemy. Even before they knew how God was going to deliver them, faith welled up inside them, and they began to praise the Lord (vv. 20-22). In Nehemiah 4, the rebuilders of the wall were being harrassed and greatly opposed by their enemies. In the middle of chapter 5, they received a word from God and they had themselves an impromptu praise gathering. In chapter 6, the wall was finished.

The timeliness of praise involves giving thanks to the Lord *prior to* deliverance. Then our praise actually becomes an expression of faith, without which it is impossible to please God (Heb. 11:6).

Praise is also the means by which faith is solidified in our hearts. If we have faith within us concerning a certain situation, we must begin to praise, or soon our faith may weaken and even be lost. It is so important that we praise *before* we see the results. We should proclaim, "Father, thank you and praise you that this matter is settled; I praise you for your Word, which never fails!" We must not wait until after the matter is settled to begin praise. Faith moves the mechanism of heaven: Praise expresses and strengthens that faith, even in the face of the most difficult problems, which often are not situational, but of a personal nature. Circumstances can change rapidly, but when one has been hurt, abused, offended, or misused, the problem seems unduly tenacious. Even prayer often brings no relief. When we find ourselves in this situation, we must learn to praise instead of murmuring, complaining, or becoming bitter.

Belief in God allows us to say, "Lord, you are never wrong, you doeth all things well. I receive this from your hand and praise you." Praising God in this manner takes our focus off earthly concerns and transports us to heavenly spheres, linking us to the One to whom we pay homage. We enter the influence of His perspective. Many a life filled with hurt, anger, and resentment has been transformed by the simple act of regular praise. I have seen countenances changed and frowns turned to smiles as a result of praise and as past experiences are left powerless in the wake of belief in the goodness of the Lord.

In 1 Corinthians 13:12, Paul said, "For now we see in a mirror dimly, but then face to face; now I know in part; but then I shall know fully just as I also have been fully known." In this life we see dimly, as if looking into a mirror covered with steam: the image is blurred and the details are obscure. Therefore, we do not understand all the ways of God in our lives, and as a result, our faith, and praise falter. This also explains the great abundance of praise in heaven. In heaven there is a perfect knowledge of the Lord and perfect understanding of His dealings in our life, and, as a result, perfect praise permeates heaven. Someday we will see with crystal clarity the purpose behind the Holy Spirit's discipline in our life and the times when our life took an unusual bend in direction. All questions will be answered and all problems solved. There will be no doubt as to the wisdom and counsel of the Lord. To the extent that we are able to see through "eyes of faith" what we will someday see in heaven, so will be the condition of our praise life. If we perceived only with our physical eyes, we would be men most miserable. Through our spiritual eyes, we are able to understand and discern the dealings of God in our lives.

To simply say that we believe in God can be a trite, often misleading statement. The demons also believe—and tremble (James 2:19). Believing in God must involve placing our trust in Him. It involves a change of life style as we desire to become like Him. If belief in God always precedes praise, it could be said that praise is an evidence of faith. Find a person who *regularly* enters true praise and you will be observing a person of faith. Lack of praise in an individual is likewise indicative of a lack of faith. The joy of the Lord is for those who have both!

10
Overcoming Through Praise

Saul had made it very clear to everyone involved that his intention was to put David to death (1 Sam. 19:1). Saul was so reprobate in his mind and actions that an evil spirit was on him and controlled him even to the point of committing murder (v. 10). Saul became enraged at his daughter for her helping David to escape. With anger he commanded his servants to go to Naioth in Ramah and to take David. The conclusion to this episode is rather amazing:

> Then Saul sent messengers to take David; but when they saw the company of the prophets prophesying, with Samuel standing and presiding over them, the Spirit of God came upon the messengers of Saul, and they also prophesied. And when it was told Saul, he sent other messengers, and they also prophesied. So Saul sent messengers again the third time, and they also prophesied. Then he himself went to Ramah, and came as far as the large well that is in Secu; and he asked and said, "Where are Samuel and

David?" And someone said, "Behold, they are at Naioth in Ramah." And he proceeded there to Naioth in Ramah; and the Spirit of God came upon him also, so that he went along prophesying continually, until he came to Naioth in Ramah. And he also stripped off his clothes, and he too prophesied before Samuel and lay down naked all that day and all that night. Therefore they say, "Is Saul also among the prophets?" (1 Sam. 19:20-24).

The same man who was filled with ungodliness for the first twenty-two verses of this chapter was controlled by the Spirit of God in the final two verses, even to the extent that he lay naked before the Lord all day and all night. In this passage of Scripture we have a fascinating account of how a great spirit of praise and worship was adequately used in subduing the evil intentions of ungodly men.

When David fled Saul's presence, he went to the man of God, Samuel the prophet. When Samuel was apprised of the situation, he did not make arrangements for David to flee the territory, nor did he call out armed men; instead, he remained right where he was and began praising God.

Samuel and the company of prophets began to prophesy. Just exactly what transpired during that extended period of time we do not know, but we do know that the Spirit of God fell upon them and they were overcome with a holy presence. My personal conviction is that they were not foretelling the future during that entire time, although that might have been included, but rather that they were praising and worshiping God under an unusual anointing of the Lord. There are several other related Scriptures which imply that prophesying involved praise, and probably the use of musical instruments.

> Afterward you will come to the hill of God where the Philistine garrison is; and it shall be as soon as you have come there to the city, you will meet a group of prophets coming down from the high place with harp, tambourine, flute, and a lyre before them, and they will be prophesying (1 Sam. 10:5).

> Moreover, David and the commanders of the army set apart for the service some of the sons of Asaph and of Heman and of Jeduthun, who were to prophesy with lyres, harps and cymbals (1 Chron. 25:1).

When the messengers of Saul came into their presence, they were overcome with this awesome spirit of praise. They quickly forgot their evil assignment and they also prophesied. Even when Saul arrived, actually before he arrived, this same powerful spirit subdued him and he was powerless to do anything but that which was honoring to the Lord.

I have seen this same miracle happen in worship services in the New Testament church. People usually enter a worship service with all sorts of thoughts in their minds, most of them foreign or even contrary to the things of the Lord. Though it is impossible to determine, I imagine many people enter the sanctuary in the flesh rather than controlled by the Spirit of God. (Of course, the Lord is always cognizant of our spiritual state.) However, when there is a great expression of God in the church, it will take precedence over any other spirit or attitude that may be present. The Christian who is out of tune with the Spirit, even the lost person, will be captivated with the praises of God's people. Psalm 22:3 tells us that the Lord Jesus is enthroned upon praises. When He is praised, His Lordship is released and it becomes predominant over all other forces.

This is why it is so important that our worship services be dynamic. The Psalmist wrote, "Great is the Lord, and greatly to be praised." It would be inconsistent to offer mediocre praise to such a great God. Christ said, "If I be lifted up I will draw all men unto Me." The best way to lift Christ up is through our praise—but it must be done in such a way as to magnify Him and do His character justice.

It is important to note that, in this biblical account, Samuel and his prophets were in a position to immediately enter worship. They were the leaders. The same must be true in our experience. Ideally, all of the church should be prepared for worship, but that is usually not the case. There must be a person or a group of people—perhaps the worship leader, the pastor, or the choir—who are wholly devoted to the task of worship, and are unquestionably prepared to lead the people, by example, into worship. It often only takes one, but, obviously, the more the better.

Our praise and worship must be so intense, yet so liberating, that it literally captivates people as they come into our midst. The influence of the devil and the flesh should be rendered powerless. This is one reason our services must begin with great praise. Save the announcements until the end of the service; welcome the visitors by sharing with them the praise of God. Whatever we do, we must create such an atmosphere of celebration that God is free to move in power, and the sooner the better.

Job described the greatness of God as revealed in nature:

> He stretches out the north over empty space, and hangs the earth on nothing. He wraps up the waters in His clouds . . . He obscures the face of the full moon . . . he quieted the sea with His power . . . by His breath the heavens are cleared (Job 26:7-130.

Yet he said:

> Behold, these are the fringes of his ways; and how faint a word we hear of Him! But His mighty thunder, who can understand (v. 14).

Do you know what the mighty thunder of God us? It is the church! The magnificence of nature only reveals the whisper of God; the church is to represent His thunder!

The church must make her praise and worship grand. There must be a great spirit of praise every time we gather together. If there is, we can be assured that God will have His way in our midst.

11
Judah—The Tribe of Praise

Genesis is the book of beginnings. Within its chapters is the initial establishment of many of the precious truths seen throughout the Bible. The foundation of each of these truths, as seen in Genesis, is usually culminated in the book of Revelation. The ministry of praise is no exception. The first mention of praise in the Bible is recorded in Genesis 29. In this account, Judah was forever established as a man of praise, and his tribe as the tribe of praise.

Jacob had two wives, Rachel and Leah, but he preferred Rachel. Jacob's hatred (29:31) of Leah was probably due to the treacherous manner in which her father, Laban, tricked Jacob into marrying Leah before he could marry Rachel.

Nevertheless, God had mercy on Leah and allowed her to bear sons to Jacob, whereas Rachel was barren. With the birth of each son, Leah hoped to gain the favor and love of her husband. She even named her third-born "Levi" (literally "attached to"), saying, "Now my husband will become attached to me, because I have borne him three sons" (v. 34).

In verse 35 the birth of her fourth son is recorded: "And she conceived again and bore a son and said, 'This time I will praise the Lord.' Therefore she named him Judah" (Hebrew *Jadah*, related to Judah). The name Judah means "praise." To study his life and the experiences of the tribe he fathered gives us great insight into principles of praise.

Judah was the fourth son of Jacob and became the leader of his brothers. It was Judah who insisted that his brother Joseph be sold into slavery instead of being murdered; during the ordeal in Egypt when Joseph was the unrecognized official of Egypt, it was judah who wanted to be kept prisoner instead of his younger brother, Benjamin. When it came time to bestow the privilege of birthright, Jacob chose Judah over his three older brothers. The blessing of this birthright gives us keep perception of the life of Judah—and consequently the life of those who praise and worship God.

When Israel was near the end of his life, he summoned all his sons to tell them what would befall them at the "end of the days" (Gen. 49). One at a time he prophesied to his sons. When it was Judah's turn, he said:

Judah, your brothers shall praise you.

It was through the tribe of Judah that the Messiah came. Our praise of Jesus is a fulfillment of this statement.

Your hand shall be on the neck of your enemies.

Judah would be victorious and successful in war. This was literally fulfilled through the life of David and is continually fulfilled as we use praise to defeat the enemy.

Your father's sons shall bow down to you.

Judah was the lawgiver (Ps. 60:7), and his was the leading

Judah—The Tribe of Praise

tribe through the wilderness experience and in the conquest of Canaan (Judg. 1:2). It is interesting to note that his brothers would both bow down to him and praise him, indicating a cheerful state of submission.

Judah is a lion's whelp.

The lion is the king of the beasts. In Revelation 5:5, Jesus is referred to as the Lion of the tribe of Judah who has overcome and is worthy to open the book. Praise will give us a boldness which we will not experience otherwise.

> The scepter shall not depart from Judah, nor the ruler's staff from between his feet, until Shiloh comes, and to him shall be the obedience of the peoples.

It is thrilling to know that on his deathbed Jacob could see the establishment of authority and government through the seed of Judah. That authority began in David when he became king, and culminated in Christ (Shiloh). Those who are well-versed in praise, and incorporate it in their daily lives, enjoy a measure of "kingdom authority" which is rightfully ours through Christ.

> He ties his foal to the vine, and his donkey's colt to the choice vine; he washes his garments in wine, and his robes in the blood of grapes; His eyes are dull from wine, and his teeth white from milk.

These verses speak of the abounding fruitfulness of the tribe of Judah, with grapevines so strong that donkeys could be tied to them, and the fruit of the vine in such abundance that the wash could be cleaned in wine.

In Christ, we have an abundance of all that is nourishing and refreshing to the soul and in our praise of Christ we draw upon that nourishment.

Another tremendous insight regarding praise is gained when we study the anointing of David as king. The chronology involved in David's kingship is very important. In 1 Samuel 15, the Bible says that God rejected Saul as king because of his disobedience. Samuel was instructed to go to the house of Jesse, where, after a rather miraculous selection process, he anointed David as king.

The tribe of Judah—the tribe of praise—was the first tribe to acknowledge the kingship of David. In 2 Samuel 2:4 it is recorded, "Then the men of Judah came and there anointed David king over the house of Judah." David was a type of Christ, and as such, there is a great lesson to be learned from this incident in his life.

Jesus is Lord. That fact has been forever established. He is the Lord of your life, the Lord of your church, your city, of all world affairs. He is Lord! However, He is not acknowledged as Lord by everyone; in fact, very few submit entirely to His Kingship. This does not diminish His authority or dominion at all; it simply frustrates the ways and plans of those unwilling to confess His rightful position.

As it was in the life of David, so it is in our experience with Christ. Just as the tribe of praise was the first to acknowledge the kingship of David, those who enter praise and worship more quickly and clearly see the Lordship of Jesus first and are in a better position to respond to His will. When we are truly worshiping God, lying prostrate at His feet (literally, or in our hearts), there is little doubt as to our allegiance to Him. If we praise Him in the congregation, it is a public demonstration of our commitment to His person

Judah—The Tribe of Praise

and His ways. One well-versed in the ways and means of worship will usually possess an uncanny ability to see the work of God in the midst of any given set of circumstances. Seeing His Lordship through spiritual eyes, he will possess a quiet rest within his spirit. He will see the hand of God at work when others only see the frustrated works of man.

I have often asked which type of service Jesus would enjoy the most, and in which He would most likely express himself in powerful ways: a service void of praise, or a service vibrant and overflowing with the praises of God's people. Which type of service would attract the lost person or the backslider and point him to Christ? The people who make praise an integral part of their lives will know more of the Lordship of Christ, will enjoy His presence more, and will attract others to His glorious life.

12
Pouring Out Offerings to the Lord

It is unfortunate that when we enter the presence of God, either corporately or individually, we are usually in a receiving mode, only interested in what we can receive from the Lord. We often fall into a "give me" syndrome. We can identify with the disappointment the Father must feel with this attitude by recalling how we feel when, having returned from a long trip, our young children are only interested in what we have brought them. It is imperative that we change our mindset when entering His presence. How pleased the Lord would be if our goal in worship was to give to Him! To give back what He has given us, to give Him those things we consider precious, to offer Him our desires and aspirations: these are areas of worship which honor and please Him.

We often fail to realize the basic implication of the tabernacle worship among the children of Israel. Their worship was centered around the ministry of the tabernacle, the place where God promised He would meet them (Exod. 25:8). Notice, however, that only the priests were allowed to enter the courts—the general population was not present. When the priests began their priestly duties inside the court, were they ministering to the people? Were they ministering to each other? They were ministering to the Lord!

> And I will sanctify the tabernacle of the congregation, and the altar: I will sanctify also both Aaron and his sons, *to minister to me* in the priest's office (Exod. 29:44 KJV; italics added).

> My sons, do not be negligent now, for the Lord has chosen you to stand before Him, *to minister to Him,* and to be His ministers and burn incense (2 Chron. 29:11; italics added).

The angels of glory also minister to the Lord: "Then the devil left him; and behold, angels came and began to minister to Him" (Matt. 4:11); and it was also a part of the early church experience; "And while they were ministering to the Lord and fasting, the Holy Spirit said . . ." (Acts 13:2 KJV).

The concept of "pouring out offerings" is a vital part of ministering to the Lord. There are four instances recorded in the Scriptures which vividly illustrate the principle of "pouring out" as we minister to the Lord. The first is in 2 Samuel 23 and concerns King David and three of his mighty men of valor.

During a time of war, David was residing in the cave of Adullum when three of his mighty men came to see him. David mentioned, probably just in passing, that he would love to have a drink of water from the well of Bethlehem, which at that time was in enemy territory. Unknown to David, the three mighty men, swords in hand, broke through the camp of the Philistines, drew water from the well, and brought it to David.

Pouring Out Offerings to the Lord

David, no doubt, was shocked and bewildered by this display of love, loyalty, and courage. Because of the danger involved in acquiring the water, David likened it to the blood of these men who had jeopardized their lives that his thirst might be quenched. Instead of drinking the water, he poured it out on the ground as a drink offering to the Lord. He worshiped God!

Some may wonder if this offended these three men, but I am sure they saw the greater significance of what David did. He had such tender regard for their lives that to drink the water would have cheapened their sacrifice and only satisfied a temporary fleshly desire. Instead, David honored God with the water. Water purchased at this price was too precious for drinking; it was only fitting that it be poured out to God as a drink offering.

In this instance, we see David pouring out to God in worship that which was precious to Him and that which was acquired through much sacrifice. Another lesson is to be learned here as we consider David's high regard for the water/blood of these men. In like manner we should hold in high honor and value the benefits gained by the blood of Jesus, shed on Calvary. Indeed, we should offer them back to God as precious and holy.

Luke 7 tells a very touching story of a sinful woman who came to worship Jesus, and who, after pouring herself out to Him, left His presence a clean, forgiven lady.

Jesus was dining at the house of Simon the Pharisee. Suddenly a prostitute entered the house uninvited and unannounced, and began to minister to the Lord. She stood behind Him, wept profusely, began to wet His feet with her tears, wipe them with her hair, and anoint them with a costly vial of perfume. What a picture of humility and repentance!

This woman was broken and was pouring her heart out to Jesus.

The host of the dinner began to accuse the woman in his heart and even questioned the Lord's understanding of the situation. The Lord sufficiently dealt with his evil thoughts and put him in his rightful place by comparing the welcome offered Him by the Pharisee with that given by the immoral woman!

> You gave me no water for My feet, but she was wet My feet with her tears.
>
> You gave Me no kiss, but she, since the time I came in, has not ceased to kiss My feet.
>
> You did not anoint My head with oil, but she anointed My feet with perfume (Luke 7:44-46).

This lady came to Jesus to give—not to receive. It is not recorded that she ever said a word. She poured out her tears, she died to herself, and she poured out her costly perfume. This chapter ends not with a word to the host, but with the Lord saying to her, "Your sins have been forgiven . . . your faith has saved you; go in peace."

In the gospels of Matthew (ch. 26), Mark (ch. 14), and John (ch. 12), a similar story is told about an entirely different woman named Mary, who was the sister of Martha and Lazarus. From all that we know of Mary, she was a God-fearing believer. The Lord often stayed at their house.

In this particular account, Mary, Martha, Lazarus, Jesus, and others were dining at the house of Simon the Leper. Mary took an alabaster vial of very costly perfume and began to pour it out on the head and feet of Jesus, wiping His feet with her hair. Some of the disciples, Judas in particular, beame indignant over the apparent waste, saying

Pouring Out Offerings to the Lord

that the perfume could have been sold and the funds given to the poor. Again, the Lord expressed His approval of such behavior by rebuking the disciples, and commending Mary. In reward for pouring out what was precious to her, "wherever the gospel is preached in the whole world, what this woman has done shall also be spoken of in memory of her." Her deed was recorded in the eternal, written Word of God!

Mary's sacrifice was very costly. John's account says that the perfume was valued in excess of three hundred denarii, which was equivalent to almost a year's wages. Many would call it a waste; but was that perfume best used on the blessed Son of God, or on human flesh? Was it best used to anoint the Holy Jesus for His impending death, or to enhance the fragrance of women in their daily routine?

The finest example of any spiritual truth lies in the person and practice of Jesus. Philippians says, He "emptied Himself taking the form of a bondservant . . . He humbled Himself by becoming obedient to the point of death" (vv. 2:7-8). On Calvary, Christ poured himself out in worship to the Father. He died to himself, offered the most costly sacrifice of eternity, and the Father was pleased. "Therefore God has highly exalted Him, and bestowed on Him the name which is above every name, that at the name of Jesus every knee should bow . . ."

When we come into the house of the Lord to worship, we must come prepared to pour ourselves out to the Lord. All that He has given us we must pour back to Him in worship; all of our rights we must relinquish to Him; all our desires, belongings and hopes for the future, we must give Him. Many saints carry feelings of hatred, guilt, resentment, and bitterness. Just think of all the frustrated feelings the sinful woman brought with her as she poured out her tears on the feet of Jesus. All those years of being misused and humiliated disappeared as the Lord forgave and cleansed her and restored her dignity.

Marvelous things will happen to us, and worship will reach new heights, when we determine in our hearts to meet with God for the purpose of pouring ourselves out to Him; not to receive from His hand, but to give to Him. The Lord desires our fellowship and love. Is it possible that I in my wretchedness could minister to the Lord? Is it true that I can give Him delight and satisfaction? I pray that I will be counted among those descendants of David whom God has called to this special ministry.

> As the host of heaven cannot be counted, and the sand of the sea cannot be measured, so I will multiply the descendants of David My servant, and the Levites who minister to Me (Jer. 33:22).

13
Thy Praise Shall Continually Be in My Mouth

It is important for us to realize that the object of our praise and worship is God himself, His character, nature, and ways. The Bible says that His ways are perfect and that His immaculate character never changes. Because of this, our praise should be constant.

Many saints succumb to the erroneous practice of praising God when they feel like it, or when they approve of His dealings in their lives. In so doing, they subconsciously put God on a performance basis and become the judge of His actions. We must learn to praise the Lord regardless of circumstances or feelings. It is quite an easy thing to praise Him when we get a promotion, a child is healed, the sun is shining, or when we can feel His presence. But what about when we lose our job, a young child is taken in death, the sky is overcast, or we go for months without sensing His direction? It is my conviction that God will inevitably lead His loved ones into a period of life when all emotional and circumstantial props are removed and the child of God must continue in his walk solely on the basis of faith in God. When this happens, praise can become an expression of faith. During those trying times, we can express our trust in the Lord by praising Him. This was the posture of Paul and Silas when, after being beaten and thrown into prison, they began singing hymns of praise to God (Acts 16:25).

The real issue behind "praising the Lord at all times" is the fact that praise must be a function of our will; it must be a volitional act. Within our soul we have our mind, will and emotions. Our mind functions in memory, understanding, and calculation. If our praise originates in our minds, we will only praise Him if we understand His ways, or if we can figure out what He is doing. The emotional element consists of our feelings and sentiments. If praise is regulated by our emotions, we will only praise Him when we feel like it—a very dangerous position. The will is our decision-making member. Some consider it the pivot point of our entire being. God has made each man's will independent, so that he may make his own choices. It is within this part of the soul that praise must be determined. We must once for all settle the issue that we *will* praise God. Regardless of how we feel or what we understand, as an act of our volition, we *will* praise God. The Lord is very pleased with this decision.

This is not to say that praise should be unemotional or that praising God for something we understand with our minds is wrong. We simply must understand that pure, unaffected praise is a decision to be made, based on our faith in God. Many times we hear the psalmist say, "I will praise the Lord." David did not say, "I feel like praising the Lord," but rather, "I *will.*" Indeed, the Psalms represent the good times and the bad times of the life of David. He had made up his mind that praise was going to be an incessant part of his life; he willed it to be so!

Closely related to this particular aspect of praise is the

concept of optimism and pessimism. The statement is often made "He is a born optimist" or "He is a born pessimist." Both are deceptions of Satan. We are not born pessimistic; at some point in life we choose to be pessimistic in nature and we daily reinforce that tragic attitude. Likewise, many choose to be optimistic—when life gives them lemons, they make lemonade. Nowhere in Scripture can one find harmony between the Spirit-controlled life and the characteristics of a pessimist. They are diametrically opposed. God desires that we be joyful and that our joy be consistent.

I recently counseled a woman who was experiencing some troubled times. An unwanted divorce had left her with two children to care for and other hardships relating to the separation. At the close of the session, I asked her what she would do if I were a medical doctor and prescribed a medicine for her to take. She replied that she would promptly purchase the medicine and take it as directed. I explained to her that although my doctorate was not in medicine, I had a prescription for her and that I expected her to follow it explictly. I instructed her to set aside some time, three times a day, to spend praising God; not reading the Bible or praying—she was to continue doing those at other times—but merely in praising God. I told her God would lead her into praise. Within a week I could see a marked improvement in her attitude; after another week her countenance had lightened. Some Sundays later I saw her and her ex-husband sitting together in church. It is amazing how therapeutic praise can be!

Several passages in the gospel of Matthew show us the importance of praising and worshiping God even when circumstances are difficult. The people described in these accounts had very real needs in their lives; many of them were heartbroken over a loved one, some had physical infirmities. But they all approached the Lord as worshipers and God met their needs.

> When he was come down from the mountain, great multitudes followed him. And, behold, there came a leper and worshipped him, saying, Lord, if thou wilt, thou canst make me clean (Matt. 8:1, 2 KJV).

> While he spake these things unto them, behold, there came a certain ruler, and worshipped him, saying, My daughter is even now dead: but come and lay thy hand upon her, and she shall live (Matt. 9:18 KJV).

> And, behold, a woman of Canaan came out of the same coasts, and cried unto him, saying, Have mercy on me, O Lord, thou son of David; my daughter is grievously vexed with a devil . . . Then came she and worshipped him, saying, Lord, help me (Matt. 15:22, 25 KJV).

> The servant therefore fell down, and worshipped him, saying, Lord, have patience with me, and I will pay thee all (Matt. 18:26 KJV).

When we have a problem we often begin to plead with the Lord. We beckon and cajole Him to help us; we logically argue our case. We act as if God is not already aware of the trial of our faith. However, God is pleased and motivated by our worship. Though it may be a shallow type of worship (which was probably the case in some of the gospel accounts), God is delighted that we come to Him in a posture of worship.

When we praise God in the midst of trying circumstances, quite often the trials will soon be eliminated. Accepting our praise as an act of faith, the Lord will act strongly on our behalf. However, this must not be our motivation for beginning to praise, nor must our praise cease if the circumstances stay the same!

Therefore, it is significant that the psalmist said, "Thy praise shall continually be in my mouth" (Ps. 34:1), and that Paul stated that we should be "always giving thanks for all things" (see Eph. 5:20; 1 Thess. 5:18). If our praise is focused on the unchanging One from whom all good things come, our praise will be unceasing, uninterrupted, and unchanging. What blissful people we will be! May our heart's cry and the living testimony of our lives be that of the prophet Habakkuk when he said:

> Though the fig tree should not blossom, and there be no fruit on the vines, though the yield of the olive should fail, and the fields produce no food, though the flock should be cut off from the fold, and there be no cattle in the stalls, yet I will exult in the Lord, I will rejoice in the God of my salvation (Hab. 3:17, 18).

14
He Made Us to Praise Him

God is most glorified, and man is at his best, when we are praising God. There is not anything a child of God can do in life that is as appropriate or more beneficial than to spend time in praising Him. As redeemed children, it is the best activity we can be involved in. There is never a time of day in which praise is improper; there is never an occasion in which praise is not apropos. Praise is adaptable to all ages: children delight in its joy, and the elderly testify with assurance of the greatness and faithfulness of the Lord. The Bible says it this way: "Praise is becoming to the upright" (Ps. 33:1).

The Hebrew word *naveh* is translated "becoming." It can also be translated "suitable, seemly, becoming, at home." The phrase has certain implications toward proper attire and proper appearance. In other words, praise is the suitable clothing for a Christian; it makes his appearance appropriate! We should be able to recognize fellow Christians because they are clothed with the garment of praise (Isa. 61:3). I sometimes ask an audience, "How many have the joy of the Lord in your heart?" to which most answer in the affirmative. The follow-up statement is a mild rebuke, "Then some of you need your heart to inform your face." One would think God had forsaken them (though He says He never will). Worldwide evangelism would experience a great wave of success if Christians would just start looking like they are supposed to look. If we all began to speak what we are supposed to speak (the praise of God), our world would be drastically changed. What do *you* wear from day to day: the garland of ashes or the mantle of praise?

The Bible states that praise is befitting to the righteous, but in our assembling together we often look upon those who are enjoying praise as odd balls, when actually in God's sight they are the norm and those not engaged in praise are acting unseemly.

I love to hear folks brag on Jesus! We need more of that in our worship services. Newspaper editorials are interesting, but what really intrigues us is the news—news about people. In our worship services, the preaching is like an editorial, but what we also need to hear is the news—what is happening in the lives of people. The testimony of saints, telling how God is working in their lives, gives validity to the preaching. It is living proof that what is being taught really works on a day-to-day basis. Next to the Word of God, there is nothing more powerful and authoritative than a personal testimony.

Sometimes a few Spirit-prompted testimonies were all that was needed for the Lord to minister in a service. More singing or preaching would have hindered the Spirit's work. Praise is becoming to the saints of God, and for this task they have been called. God proclaims through Isaiah, "the people whom I formed for Myself, will declare My praise."

He Made Us to Praise Him

If God's people will not praise Him, then who will? Will the heathen rejoice in the Lord? Will the infidel offer a sacrifice of praise to God? Praise is our privilege and right, but we must also feel a sense of compulsion and obligation in our praise life. Jesus issued a strong rebuke to a group of Pharisees who had asked the Lord to quiet down a group of His disciples who were "praising God joyfully with a loud voice." His reply to their request was, "If these become silent, the stones will cry out!" (Luke 19:37-40). The Lord is to be praised; He will be praised. If the children of God, because of apathy or hardness of heart, do not offer praise to Him, He will raise up inanimate objects to bid Him homage. What a terrible reprimand it would be if, looking into our midst, the Lord found our praise inadequate and therefore had to look elsewhere for a source of adoration.

Not only are we the principal administrators of praise in the Kingdom, but God is the only worthy recipient of praise and worship in the entire universe. Deuteronomy 10:21 says, "He is your praise, and He is your God." It has often been said that we praise God for what He does for us, His works among men, and we worship Him for who He is, His character and His attributes. I beleive there is some truth to this, though the lines cannot always be drawn so exactly. In this sense, that praise is based on works, I suppose it is permissible to praise one another, particularly if we are complimenting godliness and obedience. But when we talk in terms of worship, adoration, devotion, paying homage, or offering sacrifices—there is only one whom we worship: God. I personally like to reserve the term "praise" for reference to the Trinity. God has exclusive rights to our adoration. He is our praise.

We should have the same single focus concerning the

instruments we have been given. Second Chronicles 7:6 says, "And the priests stood at their posts and the Levites, with the instruments of music to the Lord, which King David had made for giving praise to the Lord." Those instruments had a holy purpose. They were made for one reason—to be used in the service of worship. Through the years, God has totally removed from my heart the desire to use my instrument for anything but His holy purpose. I have no desire to sing other than the songs of Zion. Though other music is acceptable, if it qualifies according to Philippians 4:8, our instruments are at their best when used for furthering the Kingdom.

Yes, He made us to praise Him. First Peter 2:9 states this with unquestionable clarity:

> But you are a chosen race, a royal priesthood, a holy nation, a people for God's own possession, that you may proclaim the excellencies of Him who has called you out of darkness into His marvelous light.

This verse teaches us that we have been chosen out of all the peoples of the earth; we have been made authoritative worshipers, equal in stature to the Levitical priest; we have been sanctified and made holy; and we are considered God's own people. The transition word "that" leads from the description of who we are to the purpose for which we exist! God has made us who we are; He has equipped us; He has nurtured and put us in working order for one purpose: to show forth the excellencies of Him who called us.

The time has come for Christians to get zealously involved in this ministry of praise. It is our trademark; it should be normal activity for us. We should be enamored with the worship of God. The Ark of the Covenant always represents the presence of God among His people. When David returned the ark to Jerusalem, he made it a priority to appoint some of the Levites as ministers before the ark (1 Chron. 16). These men worked in shifts in order to *continually* (vv. 6 and 37) offer praise to the Lord. The priests blew trumpets before the ark and used many other types of instruments in their praise. Asaph, the chief musician, had as his sole responsibility the administration of this magnificent praise. To the children of Israel, praise was not an infrequent phenomenon—it was their life. So it should be with us.

Truly, we are a people set apart to proclaim His excellence. May the words of the psalmist be our heart's cry:

> The dead do not praise the Lord, nor do any who go down into silence; but as for us, we will bless the Lord from this time forth and forever. Praise the Lord! (Ps. 115:17-18).

15
On Earth as It Is in Heaven

When the disciples asked the Lord to teach them to pray, He did not lecture on the ways and means of prayer but rather taught them a model prayer complete in both form and content. Its first three statements address the greatness and glory of God; the second trilogy has to do with our needs: past (forgive us our debts), present (give us this day our daily bread), and future (lead us not into temptation).

The Lord's third statement is the focus of this discussion. "Thy will be done, on earth as it is in heaven" (Matt. 6:10). With this one simple thought, the Lord has given us the key to discovering His will for our lives.

What makes this earth a little like heaven is God's will being done here, as it is always being done in heaven. There is no rebellion, no insurrection in heaven; God's will is obeyed the moment it is expressed. To know and obey His will, we must simply look into what is going on in heaven, and do here what is going on there. That may seem rather abstract, but it is totally feasible through prayer and Bible study.

The book of Revelation gives us the most explicit view of heaven. In reading through it, one thing becomes undeniably obvious: heaven is full of the vibrant, incessant praises of God. If one had to briefly summarize the atmosphere and the main activity of heaven, two words would suffice— praise and worship. John Newton was most accurate in proclaiming:

> When we've been there ten thousand years,
> Bright shining as the sun,
> We've no less days to sing God's praise,
> Then when we first begun.

For years we have considered Revelation a book of eschatology; but it is primarily, I think, a book of worship. When we study the book through the lens of prophecy, we oftimes get confused, argumentative, and downright defensive in regard to our particular interpretation. When we study the book through the lens of worship, our spirits are uplifted and we fall on our faces before God. If God had intended for us to understand all that has to do with the end times He could have been adequately explicit. I find great peace in knowing that when it is all over, God will be on His throne and we in His presence.

Read carefully the following passages and be captivated and enthralled with the greatness of what is happening.

> And the four living creatures, each one of them having six wings, are full of eyes around and within; and day and night they do not cease to say, "Holy, holy, holy, is the Lord God, the Almighty, who was and who is and who is to come.

And when the living creatures give glory and honor and thanks to Him who sits on the throne, to Him who lives forever and ever, the twenty-four elders will fall down before Him who sits on the throne, and will worship Him who lives forever and ever, and will cast down their crowns before the throne, saying,

"Worthy art Thou, our Lord and our God, to receive glory and honor and power; for Thou didst create all things, and because of Thy will they existed, and were created." (Rev. 4:8-11).

And when He had taken the book, the four living creatures and the twenty-four elders fell down before the Lamb, having each one a harp, and golden bowls full of incense, which are the prayers of the saints; and they sang a new song, saying,

"Worthy art Thou to take the book, and to break its seals; for Thou wast slain, and didst purchase for God with Thy blood men from every tribe and tongue and people and nation. And Thou hast made them to be a kingdom and priests to our God; and they will reign upon the earth."

And I looked, and I heard the voice of many angels around the throne and the living creatures and the elders; and the number of them was myriads of myriads, and thousands of thousands, saying with a loud voice, "Worthy is the Lamb that was slain to receive power and riches and wisdom and might and honor and glory and blessing."

And every created thing which is in heaven and on the earth and under the earth and on the sea, and all things in them, I heard saying, "To Him who sits on the throne, and to the Lamb, be blessing and honor and glory and dominion forever and ever." And the four living creatures kept saying, "Amen." And the elders fell down and worshiped (Rev. 5:8-14).

And the seventh angel sounded; and there arose loud voices in heaven, saying, "The kingdom of the world has become the kingdom of our Lord, and of His Christ; and He will reign forever and ever."

And the twenty-four elders, who sit on their thrones before God, fell on their faces and worshiped God saying, "We give Thee thanks, O Lord God, the Almighty, who art and who wast, because Thou hast taken Thy great power and hast begun to reign" (Rev. 11:15-17).

After these things I heard, as it were, a loud voice of a great multitude in heaven, saying, "Hallelujah! Salvation and glory and power belong to our God."

And the twenty-four elders and the four living creatures fell down and worshiped God who sits on the throne saying, "Amen. Hallelujah!" And a voice came from the throne, saying, "Give praise to our God, all you His bond-servants, you who fear Him, the small and great."

And I heard, as it were, the voice of a great multitude and as the sound of many waters and

On Earth as It Is in Heaven

as the sound of mighty peals of thunder, saying, "Hallelujah! For the Lord our God, the Almighty, reigns" (Rev. 19:1, 4, 5, 6).

Heavenly worship is a fascinating subject. In some ways it seems very different than what we would expect. However, it obviously pleases God and it is something we will become comfortable with and even participate in. Make note of *who* worships God in heaven in these passages: twenty-four (the priestly number) elders, dressed in white garments with golden crowns on their heads (Rev. 4:4); four living creatures, each one with a different appearance—lion, calf, man and flying eagle (Rev. 4:7); myriads of angels; every created thing in heaven, on the earth, under the earth and in the sea. Notice also *how* they worship God: they continually cry aloud; they fall down before Him; they cast their crowns before the throne; they play on harps; they offer bowls of incense; they sing; they fall on their faces. In other passages observe the *sights* and *sounds* which accompany the praise and worship: from the throne proceed flashes of lightning and peals of thunder (Rev. 4:5); seven lamps of fire burn before the throne (Rev. 4:5); the foundations of the threshold tremble (Isa. 6:4); a sea of glass surrounds the throne (Rev. 4:6); the praise is very loud (Rev. 5:12, 11:15); and, at times, the temple is filled with smoke (Isa. 6:4; Rev. 15:8). And in picturing this heavenly scene see the others the Bible says are around the throne: six-winged seraphim (Isa. 6:2); those who came out of the great tribulation (Rev. 7:14); and those who were victorious over the beast and his image (Rev. 15:2).

From eternity-past, heaven has been filled with the praises of God. For eternity-future, heaven will be filled with the praises of God. Do you know what is going on in heaven right now? The Trinity is being worshiped and adored in a very grand and unapologetic fashion.

I visit with many saints who are at a loss to discover God's will for a particular area of their life. They just cannot get a clear vision of what God wants them to do. I ask them why God should reveal more to them when they are not obeying what He has already revealed. God's will for our lives is that we praise Him! He has taught us to pray, "Thy will be done, on earth as it is in heaven." Our daily lives should in some measure resemble the daily activity of heaven. No excuse can be given for pessimism or negativism. When we see, through spiritual eyes, God on His throne, surrounded by the blood-washed throng, we can do no less than live a life of thanksgiving and praise.

Have you noticed that there is not much similarity between our worship services and heavenly worship? Some folks are going to momentarily feel a little awkward when they get to heaven because they have not been practicing a life of praise here on earth. I am not implying that our services should exactly imitate what goes on in heaven; it would be futile to attempt such a thing and would probably become a hindrance to Spirit-led spontaneity. The point is, when we look into heaven, the obvious predominant activity is praise! If we pray, "Thy will be done, on earth as it is in heaven," we must, on a regular and grand basis, praise the Lord!

It continues to amaze me how praise can drastically and supernaturally change an attitude or set of circumstances. If we would but learn to praise Him! If you are facing a difficult situation, infuse that predicament with a good dose of praise! Praise Him out loud, sing, or clap;

raise your hands; quote Scripture. You will soon sense the presence of One mightier than yourself, and He can handle any situation. Yes, Father, Thy will be done on earth, in our lives, as it is being done in heaven.

16
Dancing Unto the Lord

Let them praise His name with dancing (Ps. 149:3).
Praise Him with timbrel and dancing (Ps. 150:4).

I can recall two incidents in my ministry during which spontaneous dancing took place. The first occurred behind my back, so to speak. I was directing the choir and orchestra in an enthusiastic, rather high-spirited anthem, when a lady in the audience jumped out of her seat and started dancing in the aisle. The ushers intercepted her quietly and led her to the back of the auditorium and out to the vestibule. I learned later the woman was high, but not with the Spirit. She seemingly had reversed the admonition in Ephesians 5:18. No harm was done and the incident made good material for pastoral anecdotes.

The second episode also occurred during choral praise. The choir was concluding a glorious service of praise and worship by singing "You Shall Go Out With Joy" when one of the choir just started doing his own thing right in the middle of the bass section. I could tell by his facial expression that he was totally oblivious to anyone around him, enjoying the presence of the Lord, and having a sincere worship experience. Incidentally, it offended no one.

Dancing is inarguably a legitimate means of expressing praise. Several scriptural commands and many biblical incidents support dancing in a God-honoring fashion. The critical issue, as with all public expressions of worship, is the attitude of the heart. Is the heart seeking to please and honor God, or to draw attention to itself?

Any discussion on biblical dancing would be misleading without noting the vast difference between Old Testament dancing and modern dancing. The Hebrew form of dance usually did not involve dancing by both sexes simultaneously, it was usually by woman only, with one leading (Exod. 15:20). It was accompanied by spiritual music and often took place during a national celebration. Jewish choirs would engage in processionals, marching in time with the music and perhaps using additional choreographed movements. The modern dance, in which persons of the opposite sex perform in pairs, has no precedent in the Bible. Also, sacred dancing was never used for purposes of amusement or entertainment. One of the characteristics of a captive people was that dancing ceased (Lam. 5:15); but when deliverance came, dancing was resumed (Jer. 31:4, 12, 13).

Dancing is essentially an outward expression of an inward feeling. The body depicts what the soul and spirit entertain. In ballet physical movement is used to convey a story; sign language allows the deaf to communicate. They are both types of dance in that they both communicate using bodily motions. Obviously both sensual thoughts and desires, and spiritual ones, can be transmitted.

Dancing Unto the Lord

The Bible records many instances of dancing being used in an honorable fashion:

> And David was dancing before the Lord with all his might (2 Sam. 6:14).

> And Miriam the prophetess, Aaron's sister, took the timbrel in her hand, and all the woman went out after her with timbrels and with dancing (Exod. 15:20).

> Jephthah's daughter met him with tambourines and with dancing (see Judg. 11:34).

> The women came out of all the cities of Israel, singing and dancing, to meet King Saul, with tambourines (1 Sam. 18:6).

> When the prodigal son returned there was music and dancing (see Luke 15:25).

The Bible also registers examples of dancing being used in a dishonoring way:

> The daughter of Herodias danced before them and pleased Herod (Matt. 14:6).

> Moses . . . saw the calf and the dancing; and Moses' anger burned (Exod. 32:19).

> [The Amalekites were] eating and drinking and dancing because of all the great spoil they had taken from the land of the Philistines and from the land of Judah. And David slaughtered them (1 Sam. 30:16).

The Scriptures include three Hebrew words and two Greek words translated "to dance." In Hebrew, one means "to revolve, whirl around"; another "to spring, skip about" and another, "to revolve, whirl about." One Greek word suggests a regular motion, the other singing, the same word from which we derive our word "chorus." Evidently dance in biblical times was a cheerful, exuberant expression of joy and praise. It was a way of incorporating one's entire being in a worship experience. There must have been real abandonment of self to God.

I have always been intrigued by the account of David dancing before the Lord in 2 Samuel 6 referred to above. Here was David, the esteemed King of Judah and Israel, the distinguished warrior, the prince of the nations, wildly dancing before the Lord, in sight of all the people. What a lack of inhibition! He was so wrapped up in the joy of the Lord that it really did not matter what others thought of him. Besides, he was the king; he did not follow precedents, he set precedents! He told Michal, "It was before the Lord . . . therefore I will celebrate before the Lord" (v. 21). I am praying that God will give me such abandon that I will be more concerned with doing what is pleasing to God than worrying about what is acceptable to man. I recall seeing Arthur Blessitt at a convention with several thousand people present. All of a sudden, Arthur fell face down, spread-eagled, on the platform and prayed for a while. He then got up and delivered his message. I suppose God told him in a still, small voice, "Arthur, fall down and pray," and that is what Arthur did! A good modern-day example of abandonment.

Incidentally, someone will always mock such unrestrained freedom. This chapter concludes with God's judgment on Michal's criticism of her husband's actions: "And Michal the daughter of Saul had no child to the day of her death" (v. 23).

In modern church life and practice, dancing cannot be condemned because Scripture supports the practice; however, it cannot be considered apart from other truths, especially the principles of Romans 14 and 15, and 1 Corinthians 8-10. Furthermore, in this age dancing is so strongly associated with worldly carnality and sensuality that the association may prohibit its use in Christian worship (1 Thess. 5:22).

Some forms of dance appear less likely to offend. Basic choreography can contribute greatly to a musical performance if done with good taste. A song or message is often enhanced when interpreted by sign language. The most important thing in any worship encounter is to be pure in heart and motive, and to be obedient to the Lord. If He instructs you to dance, and your heart is right, dance. If He says "Stand still and see My glory," obey Him. Dancing, particularly in private worship, can provide a means to engage the entire body in joyful praise. Next time you are all alone, turn on some Christ-honoring music and allow your body to move in simple, natural motions. It may provide a new dimension to your praise life.

17
Lifting Holy Hands Unto the Lord

Our hands are extensions of ourselves. Have you ever noticed how we use our hands to express ourselves? When we are pleased we clap our hands; when we are happy we raise our hands; when offended our hands become tense and we raise our fists. When we see someone from a distance, we wave our hands; a sign of affection is to hold hands; a handshake is not only a greeting but often a nonverbal commitment to another person. When we are puzzled we hold up our hands with our palms up; to express sadness or grief we put our hands to our face. When we become nervous our hands shake and become wet with perspiration; when satisfied we rub our hands together. The hands of a laborer are calloused, weathered, and strong; other hands are soft, yet meticulous in their ability for detail. Hands are an extension of our lives; they reveal what we do, what we are thinking, and how we feel.

The Bible places great importance on our hands. There are many Scriptures that indicate that our hands are much more than just flesh and bone.

Hands can represent a transferral or endowment of power, authority, and blessing. In Genesis 48 the laying on of hands was used to pass on a blessing and family authority. Elsewhere the laying on of hands was used in the ordination of deacons and elders (Acts 6:6), for anointing for special work (Acts 13:3), and for the receiving of gifts (2 Tim. 1:6).

Hands are used as a part of prayer. Paul wrote to Timothy, "Therefore I want the men in every place to pray, lifting up holy hands . . ." (1 Tim. 2:8). David prayed, "Hear the voice of my supplications when I cry to Thee for help, when I lift up my hands toward Thy holy sanctuary" (Ps. 28:2). And Matthew records that "some children were brought to [Jesus] so that He might lay His hands on them and pray (Matt. 19:13).

Hands are often considered an indicator of the condition of the heart: "Cleanse your hands, you sinners; and purify your hearts, you double-minded" (James 4:8); "Who may ascend into the hill of the Lord? And who may stand in His holy place? He who has clean hands and a pure heart" (Ps. 24:3, 4); "The Lord has rewarded me according to my righteousness; according to the cleanness of my hands He has recompensed me" (Ps. 18:20).

Hands represent the power and control an individual has: "It is a terrifying thing to fall into the hands of the living God" (Heb. 10:31); "The Son of Man is going to be delivered into the hands of men" (Matt. 17:22); "And I give eternal life to them, and they shall never perish, and no one shall snatch them out of My hand" (John 10:28).

Healing power can be bestowed through the laying on of hands: "Paul went in to see him and after he had prayed, he laid his hands on him and healed him" (Acts 28:8);

"He laid His hands upon a few sick people and healed them" (Mark 6:5).

It is no wonder that God has given us our hands as a means of expressing praise to Him. In the same manner that our hands can be used to express various emotions, they can also be used to show our praise and as an aid to our worship experience. The psalmist said, "So I will bless Thee as long as I live; I will lift up my hands in Thy name" (Ps. 63:4); and "O clap your hands, all peoples; shout to God with the voice of joy" (Ps. 47:1).

Lifting up hands in praise must not be an isolated physical action but must be prompted by deep feelings that need to be expressed. It should be an outward expression of inward desire. If the expression is not initiated deep within our spirits, the raising of hands can be reduced to a vain show of religiosity, a desire to be "seen of men," something in which the Lord takes no delight (Matt. 6).

The actual act of raising hands can have several meanings and represent different attitudes.

1. The raising of hands is the international sign of surrender.

We are making ourselves totally defenseless and vulnerable when we lift our hands above our heads. So it is with some saints as they express a total surrender of themselves to God: they will raise their hands.

2. Raising hands can represent a posture of receiving.

Particularly when the palms are open and held high, the effect is one of receiving something from someone in a higher position. Some saints, when receiving provisions from the Lord, will symbolically represent this by lifting their hands.

3. Raised hands effectively focus attention outside ourselves and on the Lord.

Compare the one who has his arms and hands folded on his chest to the one whose arms are extended. We can often focus our attention on the Lord more rapidly and more effectively by extending our hands upward.

4. Our hands can symbolize the condition of our heart.

"Clean hands" or "guilty hands" are terms often used to express what is in our heart. Lifting hands can be a means of confession or a statement of praise because of the cleansing power of the blood in our lives.

5. Our hands can be used to symbolically lift up Christ.

A part of the laws of religious festivals in the life of the Jews was the observance of the wave offering (Exod. 29:26; Lev. 8:27, 23:20). The priest would take a loaf of unleavened bread and a lamb without defect and would raise them above his head and wave them back and forth as a wave offering. These items were pictures of Jesus, the bread of life and the Lamb of God. The priest was actually lifting up Jesus.

Lifting up hands may not be for everyone, but it must not be forbidden for anyone. Some people feel uncomfortable doing so, and will always feel that way; they should relax in this state and not feel pressured into any type of performance. Some Christians are very comfortable in raising their hands and consider it an important part of their worship experience. They also should feel complete liberty in this means of expression.

It is my persuasion that the lifting of hands was a prevalent part of Hebrew worship. The Hebrew word *yadah* literally means "to hold out the hands, to revere or worship with extended hands." It is usually translated "to thank" in most versions of the English Bible, but there is serious doubt as to the accuracy of that particular translation (see chapter 26). Applying the literal meaning should surely change our perspective on numerous verses. Try reading the following verses with the new interpretation: 2 Samuel 22:50; 1 Chronicles 16:34; Nehemiah 12:24; Psalm 105:1, 107:1. *Yadah* is used 39 times in the Old Testament; the Israelites did a lot of hand raising!

It is likewise my persuasion that among God's people the lifting of hands will and should become much more common. It is time we realize that we are bought with a price, that our hands do not belong to us. They belong to someone else, and the One who owns them will use them for His pleasure.

It is such a natural thing to use our hands to express ourselves. Whenever I come home my two girls run to me with outstretched, raised hands. It is an expression of love that I cannot refuse. I certainly do not say, "Put those hands down; are you becoming a fanatic?" We use body language all the time—why not use it to show love for Him who died for us and who reigns eternally in the heavens?

Another such expression with our hands is clapping, by which we show joy. We applaud when we are appreciative, when we are impressed, thankful, or want to audibly respond to a certain situation. It is very common and natural to clap our hands in order to become involved in music to which we are listening. The danger in clapping in the midst of a worship service is that by our clapping we may be giving glory to a person instead of the Lord, but, apart from this, clapping is a very scriptural and effective means of worship.

Our hands are vital to the demands of everyday life. We use them constantly in our work, we use them to eat with, to write; why not use them to praise the Lord? Many will find a new sense of joy and expression in using their hands to honor Him.

18
Singing—The Christian's Right and Privilege

Music is one of the primary means that God has provided for His saints to praise and worship Him. There is something special about music. It allows us to express our hearts and spirits in a way which surpasses all other means of expression. Music also has the potential to affect others in a way which supersedes other types of communication. It can directly and simultaneously affect all three parts of the triadic nature of man: body, soul, and spirit.

Music was created by God for the express purpose of honoring and worshiping Him. As with many of God's creations, Satan has attempted, and succeeded, to adulterate its use and pervert it for his purposes. Many sincere believers fall into the trap of condoning and even participating in distorted forms of music (see chapter 21, "The Song of Fools"). Music is, of course, at its highest and best when used in the service of the Lord. It fulfills its heavenly purpose when used for the benefit of the Kingdom of God.

It is interesting to note that music pre-dated the creation of man (Job 38:7) and will be an integral part of our eternal existence in heaven (Rev. 5:8-9). This insight gives music an eternal value and demonstrates its significance to the heart and mind of God. There are so many things that we involve ourselves in day by day that will be of no value in eternity-future, and for the most part they will be nonexistent: medical, argicultural, amd monetary concerns to name a few. But music will be alive and well! When we study music and train to sharpen our musical skills, it is a long-term investment!

Music played a prominent role in the life of Old Testament worshipers. Indeed, the entire life of Israel was centered around the Temple worship. At one point in time, there were 4,000 Levites involved in the ministry of music (1 Chron. 23:5). Old Testament music included duets (Judg. 5:1); women's choruses (Exod. 15:20; 1 Sam. 18:6); men's choruses (1 Chron. 25); mixed choirs (Exod. 15; 1 Chron. 13:8); and organized choirs (1 Chron. 16:4-7; Ezra 2; Ezek. 2:41, 70). All types of instruments were used: azor, dulcimer, psaltery, harp, pipe, trumpet, cornet, organ, flute, shofar, sackbut, cymbals, and drums.

Music must be a priority of the New Testament church. It must be considered important and receive due support in all ways: adequate financial allocations must be made, trained personnel should be employed, and it should be considered an integral and essential part of the worship service. I cringe at the thought of using music to get everyone in the auditorium and quieted down, or to allow everyone to stand and stretch. Music must be seen as more important than that. I believe any church whose music ministry is lacking is likewise deficient in its ministry to its constituency.

We have been tricked and deceived into believing that only the talented or trained can sing. As a result, our churches are composed of the 20% who are involved singers, 40% who are timid contributors, and 40% who never even attempt to make a joyful noise unto the Lord. Physiologically, the same vocal mechanism used for speech is used for producing music. In essence, if a person can talk, he can sing. No excuses for those who say, "I just can't sing." Singing must be learned as must any other skill, but it can be taught to any person, regardless of age or background.

Our music must be more congregation-oriented! Perhaps the Minister of Music's primary objective should not be the development of excellent vocalists and instrumentalists but rather the encouragement and teaching of the church body as a whole. Just as in the case of the tribe of Levi, there will always be those who possess more musical expertise, are willing to develop their talent, and are called to the music ministry; but they should not be considered to the exclusion of the body at large.

A deacon in our church just returned from visiting Dr. Paul Cho's mega-church in Korea. He reported that there was great joy and rejoicing in all the worship services (ten in one Sunday!). Everyone sings, from the young to the old. The comment was even made that when someone sitting on the platform looks out over the audience and sees someone not singing during the time of praise, they assume that he is lost and they begin praying for him! That spirit of participation should permeate all our churches. The absence of music is always a sign of consternation. Where there is not the sound of music, the judgment of God has usually fallen. In Psalm 137, the lyricist said, "By the rivers of Babylon, there we sat down and wept . . . we hung our harps. . . . How can we sing the Lord's song in a foreign land?" In Revelation 18, the curse pronounced upon Babylon included, "And the sound of harpists and musicians and flute players and trumpeters will not be heard in you any longer" (v. 22). The voice of Amos the prophet declared, "I hate, I reject your festivals . . . Take away from Me the noise of your songs; I will not even listen to the sound of your harps" (Amos 5:21, 23). One of the signs of a healthy, happy church is that there is joyous singing.

One main characteristic of the life and activity of the church which distinguishes it from Old Testament temple worship is that all ministry is administered mutually. Under the New Testament, there is the priesthood of the believer (1 Pet. 2:5, 9) in which all become ministers and all are ministered to. When there is prayer, the encouragement is "Pray for one another" (James 5:16); when confession is necessary, "Confess your sins one to another" (James 5:16); when exhorting, "Exhort one another" (Heb. 3:13); when comforting, "Comfort one another" (1 Thess. 4:18). Likewise, when singing is enjoyed, it should be mututally expressed, "Teaching and admonishing one another with psalms and hymns and spiritual songs" (Col. 3:16).

Music has been given to the children of God as an instrument of praise and worship. This, of course, includes instrumental music, though I have more closely examined vocal music because it is the instrument of the masses. It has been given to all, not just a select few. I would encourage you to lay aside any fear or inhibition which may bind you, and sing unto the Lord! After all, it is the Lord to whom we sing, so let Him be the judge of how you sound. I have a feeling that He will be delighted with both your effort and the sounds which come forth from your heart and mouth.

19
Praise Him In Song

> The Lord thy God in the midst of thee is mighty; he will save, he will rejoice over thee with joy; he will rest in his love, he will joy over thee with singing (Zeph. 3:17 KJV).

God sings! What a delightful thought! When God thinks about His love for us, it impels Him to sing. When God wants to rejoice, when He wants to praise, He chooses music to express himself. Music is a part of the eternal existence of God; how wonderful that He has given us the joy of music as a tool to express godliness in our lives.

Music is the primary instrument of praise and worship. We usually devote half of our worship service to the ministry of music. Though there are other ways to express ourselves to God, music seems to provide an unlimited means of communicating our love, adoration and commitment to God. Likewise, music has an unequalled ability to penetrate and influence the body, soul, and spirit of man.

There at at least six areas in which music can be used to increase and help our spiritual lives. When we participate in music, our spirits are released, our lives can be made sensitive, we can express our most intimate feelings to God, we are cleansed, we are elevated to heavenly heights, we can teach and admonish, and our hearts are unified toward godly purposes.

Releasing Our Spirits Through Music
Lee Roy Till once defined music as "an overflow of the Christian life." There are times when we become so full of the goodness of the Lord that we are in desperate need to enunciate our gratitude. At times like these, words often seem inadequate. When our hearts demand expression, music can function as an agent of release.

I remember one evening during a revival service when the Spirit of God moved in such power and we all received a special touch of the Lord. Following the service, my family and I went home but my spirit could not be silent! I ended up out in the backyard under the trees singing praise choruses for nearly an hour. Only after my spirit had expressed itself to God could I retire for the evening.

Indeed, the passage which states "speaking to one another in psalms and hymns and spiritual songs, singing and making melody with your heart to the Lord" (Eph. 5:19) is preceded by the command to be filled with the Spirit. As we are filled with the Spirit we will sing!

Music Can Be Used to Sensitize Our Lives
It is interesting to observe that the more mature a person becomes in Christ, the more sensitive his demeanor becomes. His entire being becomes more refined:

his mannerisms, his speech, and even the way he carries himself.

In human sentiment, we have both delicate and rough feelings. We are by nature rough, hard, insensitive, sometimes crude, even awkward. The world teaches us to be hard and tough in our dealings with people; it is not concerned at all with our becoming eloquent and sensitive.

Contrary to what the world teaches, the Lord desires that we become delicate and refined. Jesus was a gentle man, always in control of himself and the circumstances around Him. John the Baptist, whom we usually think of as a rather crude individual, was actually quite eloquent and poetic in his mannerisms and speech. For example: "Behold, the Lamb of God, who takes away the sin of the world!" and "It is He who comes after me, the thong of whose sandal I am not worthy to untie" (John 1:27, 29).

Music intrinsically has the potential of developing sensitivity in musicians. As a member of the fine arts (along with drama, painting, sculpture, etc.) it concerns itself with subtleties, nuances, and detailed means of expression. By learning these traits in music, we can transfer and inculcate them into all areas of our lives. I am sure my choir wonders why we will often spend a seemingly inordinate amount of time rehearsing some small musical subtlety in a particular anthem, when, in reality, that subtlety will probably be forgotten when we perform the piece (the unfortunate result of having only one rehearsal per week). What I am trying to develop is not just one isolated musical idea, but sensitivity in my singers.

Music Allows Us to Express Our Most Intimate Feelings to God and Others

The modern gospel song is usually concerned with communicating a personal experience from the life of the lyricist. There are many instances in Scripture where similar songs were sung:

> Song of Moses (Exod. 15)—After God delivered the Israelites from the Egyptians.
>
> Song of Deborah (Judg. 5)—After God had delivered Israel from Sisera, the commander of King Jabin's army.
>
> Song of Hannah (1 Sam. 2)—When Samuel, the son that God had miraculously given her, was dedicated to the Lord.
>
> Song of David (2 Sam. 22)—When God delivered him from the hand of all his enemies and from Saul.
>
> Song of Mary (Luke 1)—When Mary and Elizabeth met and confirmed the birth of Christ.

When these individuals had very moving experiences, they wanted to relate to others their joy and gratitude. They in essence wanted to testify of God's dealings in their lives. They used music to communicate and record these events and emotions.

Music Can Cleanse and Elevate Our Spirits

In Eastern lands, there was a custom known as footwashing. The combination of dusty roads and open sandals made it customary for a basin of water and towels to be made it customary for a basin of water and towels to be available at the entry-way of a home. A slave, or the visitor himself, would perform the washing in most cases, but sometimes the host might do so as a sign of special favor. The practice of foot-washing is not an active part of our society or church-life today, but "spiritual foot-washing" should be.

Though we are not of the world, we are in the world (John 17), in the sense that we are exposed to the filth and corruption around us. A Christian young person, in going to school, may hear humanistic teachings, be exposed to filthy language, and hear rock music in the locker roon. He may not participate in any of these activities or approve of them in his heart, yet he becomes "dusty" just by being exposed to them. This young person needs a spiritual foot-washing!

Music is an effective way to cleanse and elevate our spirits. When we listen to or participate in godly music, we receive a spiritual foot-washing! As we sing praises to the Lord, our spirits are washed and refreshed and we are reminded of our heavenly position with Christ (Eph. 2:6). We regain a godly perspective and the things of this world grow dim. This is one reason the mid-week service is so important. It allows us to come once again to the fountain of life and partake freely, and in so doing be refreshed for the remainder of the week.

Through Music We Can Teach and Admonish

I recently asked our congregation, during an evening service, how many could quote from memory Zephaniah 3:17, Galatians 4:6, Psalm 27:1, and other verses. I had no volunteers at first, but then I reminded them that we had all learned the verses through Scripture choruses.

One of the best ways to convey and retain a spiritual truth or Scripture is to put it to music. Just think of the mammoth treasury of theological truth which has been taught and reinforced through the singing of hymns such as: "Trust and Obey," "Holy, Holy, Holy," "To God Be the Glory," and countless others. Few sermons preached on salvation by grace versus works would be as effective as one singing of "Just As I Am." This is particularly effective with children. If they learn a Bible verse or spiritual truth by learning to sing it, it will be theirs forever.

Music Unifies

In an almost unexplainable way, music has an ability to unify. There is something significant about everyone stating the same message and doing so with musical consonance. I am sure it has something to do with the fact that our speech is a manifestation of our volition and therefore a public statement of our convictions.

When a worship service begins, people from all walks of life come together. Their background is different, their education is diverse, their most recent conversation would entail every subject imaginable. How in the world can such a varied group become unified so quickly? Through music.

When God's people sing, they are reminded of their oneness in Christ and their solidarity of purpose, and they are all encouraged, comforted and motivated regarding the things of the Lord.

One enjoyable aspect of music is that all we have to do is participate to receive all of the above-mentioned benefits. We do not need to understand the philosophy of music or even its theoretical basis. The important thing is that on a regular basis we make melody in our hearts to God. In so doing, we will be participating in one of the activities God himself enjoys!

20
Performance Standards for God's Musicians

Music belongs to God's people. God created music not so that rock bands might have a means of expressing their sensual thoughts, nor that we might entertain ourselves. The primary purpose of music in this universe is the praise and worship of God. Music is, in itself, an instrument, a tool for godly purposes, Music is a means to an end.

In Scripture, the Lord has given us certain performance standards regarding music. These give us general guidelines for the preparation and performance of music for the courts of the Lord.

God's musicians are to play skillfully.
   Play skillyfully with a shout of joy (Ps. 33:3).

> And Chenaniah, chief of the Levites, was in charge of the singing; he gave instruction in singing because he was skillful (1 Chron. 15:22).

It is interesting to note that music has its basis in natural laws of physics and acoustics. It is not something we have created or developed, but rather something we have discovered. Because of this, it is not a step of compromise but rather a measure of necessity that we submit ourselves to the laws of music. It is important that we study the theory of music and work to become proficient in its performance. For instance, there is nothing unspiritual about studying vocal pedagogy; in truth, it is necessary if we are to offer a pleasing sacarifice of praise. Indeed, if pursued with the proper motive, the study of music can become a type of spiritual preparation.

Spirituality and musical excellence do not conflict in any way. There seems to be a gross misunderstanding among some saints who think that music refined in quality loses its appeal and effectiveness. Perhaps the error lies in a misapplication of increased musical aptitude, for which professional church musicians would be at fault. Let me explain. In any field, a professional tends to gravitate toward more complicated systems in order to test and challenge an increased understanding or ability. The further he goes, the more removed he is from the laity, those who are not trained in that particular field. A computer programmer, in order to further his skills, will delve into areas far removed from the average home computer operator. Concerning music, there is no question that Bach's "St. Matthew's Passion" is a far more interesting work than a familiar gospel anthem, and, for those who can understand its intricacies, it is probably more inspiring. The only problem is that the average lay person cannot grasp the significance of such a work. However, this does not mean that the gospel anthem cannot be performed with the same skill and insistence upon quality as the great classic. Therefore, it becomes not an issue of musical quality but rather musical style. The finesse gained from years of vocal study can and must be

Performance Standards for God's Musicians

applied to a gospel song as it would be to an aria or a cantata.

Excellence is an attribute of God. It is something that we, as Christians, should strive for in all areas of life. It is not a matter of "How sloppy can we make it and God still bless it?" but rather "How good can we make it for the glory of God?" Such an attitude should prevail in all of our musical endeavors for the Lord.

In 1 Chronicles 21, King David needed a place to build an altar unto the Lord. He approached Ornan and offered to buy his threshing floor. Ornan replied, "Take it for yourself . . . I will give it all." David's response was, "No, but I will surely buy it for the full price, for I will not offer a burnt offering which costs me nothing" (vv. 23-24). We must take the same position as we prepare our music for the worship of God. We should not offer ill-prepared sacrifices of praise. They must cost us something. God deserves our best. He deserves our skillful performance.

God's musicians are to perform with all their might.
> And David and all Israel were celebrating before God with all their might (1 Chron. 13:8).

> Great is the Lord, and greatly to be praised (Ps. 48:1).

Most of us are too inhibited for our own good. The Bible does teach sobriety and moderation, but when it comes to praise, we should feel such a sense of security with the Lord that we become uninhibited. The performance of sacred music should always be approached with enthusiasm, eagerness, and zeal.

I tell my choir that on Sunday morning they should

approach their leadership responsibility in the worship service with the same fervor as a couple of hunting dogs approach their job on a crisp fall day. You do not have to force the dogs out of their cages, encourage them to run, or stimulate them in any way; it's usually quite a chore just to keep up with them!

There seems to be a strong correlation established in Psalm 48:1: to the degree that God is great, to that degree should He be praised. How great is the Lord? His greatness is infinite and unsearchable. In like manner, our praise should be with ardor and greatness.

God's musicians are to perform in unity.

> . . . and all the Levitical singers . . . and with them one hundred and twenty priests blowing trumpets, in unison when the trumpeters and the singers were to make themselves heard with one voice to praise and to glorify the Lord (2 Chron. 5:12-13).

> That with one accord you may with one voice glorify the God and Father of our Lord Jesus Christ (Rom. 15:6).

We underestimate the power and momentum which is developed when people agree on a mutual goal and then all pledge their assets and energies toward the fulfillment of that goal.

The two verses mentioned above emphasize the importance of unified praise. Several factors make this possible. We share a common goal in our praise experience: our praise has a sole recipient, the Holy Trinity. We are able to praise because the love of Christ has been shed abroad in our hearts. We have the same Spirit dwelling in us, crying "Abba, Father." This common denominator makes us one.

Before any of my ensembles perform, I try to make sure we are unified. I attempt to discern if anyone is performing for reasons of personal aggrandizement. I encourage everyone to get right before God and right with each other, and I urge them to yield to the power and control of the Holy Spirit. The performance and its effectiveness is always greatly dependent upon unity.

God's musicians are to perform with spirit and understanding.

> I will sing with the spirit, and I shall sing with the mind also (1 Cor. 14:15).

There is a two-fold emphasis in this verse. Paul instructed us to incorporate two elements in our singing: we are to sing with the spirit and with the mind. This chapter of Corinthians deals with spiritual gifts and the preference of some gifts over others. It is not a discourse on music. However, upon reaching the conclusion of his argument, Paul inserted this verse which ties in music to what he had been discussing. The essence of his argument is that public worship should be performed so as to be understood. In verse sixteen, he asked what value there is to the unbeliever, or the ones unversed in spiritual gifts, if we bless in spirit only? Paul further stated that he would rather speak five words with his mind than ten thousand words in a tongue (v. 19).

The lesson to be learned is that we must sing having been filled with the Spirit (Eph. 5:19; Col. 3:16), but we must also sing so as to communicate to those who hear us. How can one be edified or encouraged by our music if they cannot understand it? Some churches consistently perform in a musical style foreign to their audience. A wise musician learns to perform music using both his spirit and mind.

Performing music as God would have us perform is serious business. If we believe we sing to Him, then we must strive to please His ear and His musical taste. As Richard Dinwiddie has stated:

> God is not tone deaf. A perfect God must have truly "perfect pitch"—no variance of intonation ever escapes Him.
>
> He knows, for instance, whether or not the church's sanctuary piano or organ is in tune and how close the soloist really is to the melody. All too often I can imagine Him raising a divine finger before an errant singer and pleading, "G-sharp!" His ear is better than the finest conductor's. He understands fully the most sophisticated harmonic and rhythmic structures, and He hears whether or not our performances have stylistic integrity, appropriate phrasing, the right tonal color, correct tempos, and proper dynamics.
>
> Our limited insights cannot possibly approach the musical understanding of the Master Musician. Yet, on any given Sunday, our practices show that we apparently assume we have unlimited freedom to indulge personal musical prejudices in the service of God without serious reference to His views—as if what He may have to say about music could not be important.*

---

* Richard Dinwiddie, "The God Who Sings," *Christianity Today,* July 15, 1983, p. 18.

Performance Standards for God's Musicians

As always, God is, above all, interested in the attitude of our hearts. Beautiful music played to the glory of God can be ineffectual if our hearts are not right before Him. This was the situation when the prophet Amos told the Israelites, "Take away from Me the noise of your songs; I will not even listen to the sound of your harps" (Amos 5:23).

God has a standard of music: He also has performance standards for His musicians. Regardless of whether we have an abundance of talent or a minimal amount, we must strive to be in consonance with His desires; then we will fully enjoy our offering of praise and God will be pleased with our conscientiousness.

21
The Song of Fools

> It is better to listen to the rebuke of a wise man than for one to listen to the song of fools (Eccles. 7:5).

We are surrounded by foolish songs, or the "song of fools." I estimate that 80% of what is on the radio is foolish. The record-covers visually represent the perverted trash recorded on the albums. The distribution of foolish music is so profuse that often one must make a concentrated effort to avoid listening to such music. I wish I had a free meal for every time I've had to ask a waitress to turn down or, preferably, turn off the distracting music that was being played so loud as to make conversation difficult. Just as Satan has attempted to counterfeit and pollute other items in God's creation, he has taken music and, using its intrinsic power, used it to further his evil ways.

Music is powerful. It has a mystical ability to penetrate the very essence of man and to influence and control attitudes, judgments and, eventually, actions. Psychologists have discovered that by controlling certain variables in music, especially tempo and dynamics, they are able to manipulate human behavior. This is the purpose behind the canned music heard in many public buildings. In a doctor's office, soft soothing music will calm the patients. In manufacturing, production can be increased or decreased simply by changing the style of music played.

Aristotle, in his *Doctrine of Imitation,* stated:

> Music directly imitates (represents) the passion or state of the soul, hence when one listens to music that imitates a certain passion, he becomes imbued with the same passion; and if over a long time he habitually listens to the kind of music that rouses ignoble passions, his whole character will be shaped to an ignoble form. In short, if one listens to the wrong kind of music he will become the wrong kind of person.

I recall hearing Bill Gothard share how he had discipled a group of young people in the church where he was serving. As the months passed, they were gaining victory over many ungodly habits and seemed to be making good progress in their Christian walks. However, they soon reached a plateau beyond which they could not progress. For weeks there seemed to be a stronghold causing spiritual stagnation. He finally discovered that the young people, out of ignorance, had not forsaken their worldly music; it remained a daily source of spiritual compromise and an area through which Satan had access to their lives. When the records and tapes were destroyed, they received spiritual freedom and spiritual progress resumed. I believe this to be Satan's strongest suit among young people today, particularly Christian youth. So often we find Christian young people

The Song of Fools

with whom drugs are not a problem; they would not even contemplate such a thing. To them, drinking and immorality are unthinkable. But these same young people will entertain the devil's music, subject themselves to its philosophy of love and ethics, and allow it to influence their lives. The problem, of course, is not exclusive to young people. Many adults receive just as much wrong influence from country-western as young people do from rock, disco, etc. In the case of country-western, it is usually not so much the music that is offensive to God as the lyrics.

The children of light have no business listening to, and, in so doing, condoning the music of the world. Peter stated: "But you are a chosen race, a royal priesthood, a holy nation, a people for God's own possession, that you may proclaim the excellencies of Him who has called you out of darkness into His marvelous light; for you once were not a people, but now you are the people of God (1 Pet. 2:9, 10). The testimony of every saint should be, "He put a new song in my mouth, a song of praise to our God" (Ps. 40:3). That new song is the song of Jesus and His holy, sanctified kingdom. It is interesting to note that in Ecclesiastes 7:5, the verse quoted at the beginning of this chapter, the parallel statement involves listening to the rebuke of a wise man. Those who listen to the song of fools will develop a rebellious attitude and will indeed need the rebuke of a wise man. God's Word does not say it is better to study the Bible or even to listen to godly music than to listen to the song of fools. The word of warning is much more severe than that. To be rebuked is not a pleasant thing at all, and yet it is more to be desired than foolish songs.

Now to a much more exacting subject—the adaptation and utilization of worldly musical styles in the music of the church. What about Christian rock or Christian disco, many ask? The most penetrating and powerful aspect of a song lies in its musical properties and *not* in its lyrics. The use of Christian lyrics does not qualify a song as one that is pleasing to the Lord and useful in His kingdom. This was the big fallacy of many groups back in the early 70's. A rock music group would have a religious experience, many no doubt a genuine salvation experience, after which they would want to become a "Christian rock group." But only their lyrics would change. They still played with a loud, driving beat, but instead of "I love Susie," it was "I love Jesus." A mere change in words does not transform a song into one fit for the hymnbook of heaven. The spirit of a song, as created by the combination of musical factors (timbre, melody, harmony, rhythm, dynamics, tempo, range, form, etc.), determines whether it is fit for spiritual use. The lyrics are only secondary when considering the total significance communicted by a song, though, obviously, if the lyrics are carnal and immature they will ruin any musical setting, regardless of how beautiful it may be.

Borrowing musical style from worldly sources has great inherent problems. While trying to be "relevant" we usually compromise and dilute the integrity of our message. The church should produce such creative, excellent music that the world finds itself borrowing from the church.

What then are the criteria for music evaluation? How do we distinguish the "song of fools" from the "songs of Zion"? Surprisingly, the answer is quite simple, and easily implemented with quick and sure results by one who is committed to Christ and the pursuit of holiness.

First, in regard to vocal music, the lyrics must qualify according to Philippians 4:8. Are the lyrics true: are they in consonance with what God's Word teaches? Are they honorable: do they maintain the high integrity of the person of Christ? Are they pure: do they offer no offense to the holiness of God? Are they lovely: do they exhibit the graciousness of the Lord? Are they of good report: do they speak the truth in love?

Quite frankly, this first element of criteria would eliminate from our listening the majority of music played on secular airwaves. But what if the words do qualify according to Philippians 4:8; or what about pure instrumental music: on what basis can we evaluate music irrespective of words?

Bill Gothard has developed a system of evaluation based on establishing a correlation between the three basic elements of music: melody, harmony, and rhythm; and the three basic elements of man's nature: spirit, soul, and body. He theorizes that just as the spirit of man should have preeminence over the soul and body, likewise the melody should be the predominant factor in music. As the soul is in subjection to the spirit, so the harmony of a piece should support, amplify and complement the melody. Finally, the rhythm, though necessary, should play a subordinate role and not be of such nature that it draws attention to itself. There is more to Gothard's approach, but this summary gives a general idea of his approach. I agree in general with his theory, realizing though that it still leaves room for subjective judgments. I believe there is a better, more sure way.

The Bible says that we are born of the Spirit (John 3; 1 John 5); that the Spirit searches all things (1 Cor. 2:10); that we are to examine all things (1 Cor. 2:15); and that the Spirit will lead us into all truth (John 14:26). Colossians 3:15 says, "Let the peace of Christ rule in your hearts." We have the Holy One of Israel living within us, and the Holy Spirit of Truth. In any given situation, if we allow that Holy presence to reign and control, and if we leave the decision to His taste and preference, we will never lack direction. When listening to a musical selection, we need only ask: "Jesus, is this pleasing to you?"; "Do you take delight in this music?"; "If you were here in person would you be pleased, or would I be embarrassed?"; "Is this the type of music that surrounds your throne?"; "Holy Spirit, do you bear witness with these sounds?"; "Father, is this music fulfilling the holy purpose for which you created music?" As we ask these questions, the answer comes immediately to our spirits. The Spirit of God is never confused, or without answer. He is never indecisive; there is no gray area with Him. It is either light or darkness, truth or falsehood. He will lead us into all truth. Our problem, of course, is receiving His direction and submitting to the truth.

Through the years, God has totally eliminated from my heart the desire for any type of music other than the songs of Zion. I can honestly say with the Psalmist, "He has put a new song in my mouth, a song of praise to God." Our lips were redeemed that we might speak forth His praise; our ears were redeemed that we might receive into our hearts the gospel of Christ; and our hearts have been sealed by the Holy Spirit of truth and life. We are no longer attracted to the song of fools. Our testimony is: "I have no song to sing, but that of Christ my King."

22
The Lord Inhabits the Praises of His People

The best thing that can happen in any situation is for Jesus to appear on the scene. Wherever He is, everything is all right!

Consider these instances from the Gospels: A funeral procession was en route to bury a widow's only son—until Jesus arrived. Then their sorrow was turned to rejoicing as the Lord commanded the dead boy to rise (Luke 7). The host of a wedding was about to suffer embarrassment because the wine had run out—until Jesus' help was sought. Because the servants did as He instructed, the host avoided embarrassment (John 2). In Matthew 14, five thousand men plus women and children had not eaten all day. The presence of one man made the difference. Jesus was there. When He was asked to handle the situation, all needs were met. All that needs to happen in any taxing situation is for Jesus to be in residence and for His lordship to be confessed.

Have you ever been in a trying situation and paused momentarily to invite the Lord Jesus to come and be present in the situation, and to do whatever He wants to do?

It works! The Lord was present at the wedding in Cana because He was invited. Wherever Jesus is and where he is acknowledged as Lord, everything is always under control. What great comfort the disciples must have experienced walking in the presence of Jesus day after day. There must have been a calm assurance among them that everything was going to be okay. There was no situation that could come upon them but that Jesus would know exactly what to say, what to do, and how to handle the predicament.

In our daily life and walk, if we could just discover where the Lord dwells, where He abides, where His habitat is, then we too could have the assurance of His presence in power. What is God's address? Where does He manifest himself? The Psalmist tells us that the Lord inhabits the praises of His people! "But thou art holy, O Thou that inhabitest the praises of Israel" (Ps. 22:3 KJV).

Praise is the act of adoring God and His ways, declaring His worth to His face. It is in such an environment that He chooses to dwell. Another translation of this verse in Psalm 22 says, "Thou who art enthroned upon the praises of Israel" (NAS). When we praise Jesus we are placing Him on the throne; we are agreeing as to His Lordship. He is then free to be who He is among us. He is "released" to exert His power and control. Praise is our official invitation for Jesus to take charge of the situation. When God's people begin to truly worship Him in spirit and truth, Christ will soon be present—and where He is present, everything is all right.

Consider Jonah's dire predicament. Because of his disobedience, he ended up in the belly of a great fish. Jonah confessed his sin to the Lord and said, "But I with the the voice of thanksgiving will sacrifice to thee" (Jonah 2:9). While in the belly of that great fish, Jonah began to praise

The Lord Inhabits the Praises of His People

God! The very next verse states, "Then the Lord commanded the fish, and it vomited Jonah up onto the dry land." In the midst of his trouble, Jonah began to praise the Lord, and soon had the Lord himself as his companion, who quickly provided salvation.

Second Chronicles 20 tells the fascinating story of Jehoshaphat and his victory over the enemy. The sons of Moab, Ammon, and some of the Meunites came to make war against Judah. Jehoshaphat led the people to fall down before the Lord and to worship Him, and then to stand up "to praise the Lord God of Israel, with a very loud voice" (vv. 18-19). Then they began to sing a little praise chorus, "Give thanks to the Lord, for His lovingkindness is everlasting" (v. 21). When they began singing and praising, the Lord came into their midst and caused havoc and complete destruction among the enemy. It took three days to pick up the spoil.

Praise provides direct access to the presence of God. Have you ever had trouble coming into the presence of God? Often we try to enter His presence through Bible study, but experience difficulty; often through prayer, but find His presence elusive. We try to go over the fence instead of through the gate! Psalm 100 says, "Enter His gates with thanksgiving, and His courts with praise." This is the key to entering the court of the Lord. Where the high praises of God's people abound, there the Lord will be!

For us to abide continually in the presence of Jesus, our praise must be incessant. Hebrews 13:15 commands us to continually offer up a sacrifice of praise to God. Psalm 34 exhorts us to bless the Lord at all times and to keep His praise continaully in our mouths. Too many people try to praise the Lord only one day a week, on Sunday at church.

Such an attempt is futile, inconsistent, and usually leads to superficial worship. Praise must become a daily, even an hourly, yes, even a moment-by-moment experience in our lives.

Then we will begin to walk continually in the presence of the Lord. Our homes should be filled with the sweet aroma of praise; those at work should notice the aura within which we exist; those whom we contact during the day should be able to sense that we have a constant companion. When this happens in our individual lives, the time devoted to corporate praise on Sundays will become a great time of power.

God is at home in our praise. Within praise He settles down and is able to work. The life, home, or church that truly praises Him will delight in His presence and will find the Lord doing His thing among them. Theologically, we know that God is omnipresent and that He personally dwells in the life of every believer, but in reality we know that His glory and majesty are not fully manifest in every believer, and certainly not in all world circumstances. I have visited many places and stayed in many hotel rooms, but the place where I settle down, do my best work, and express myself most fully, is in my home. God is at home in praise! Indeed, He is everywhere, and of course He dwells within every believer; but He inhabits and manifests himself in the midst of praise!

How long has it been since you enjoyed His presence? Are you going through one of those times when your prayers seem to rise no higher than the ceiling, when Bible study seems to provide no nourishment, and when, in general, you just cannot feel God's presence? Such times are usually orchestrated by the Lord to teach us to walk by

The Lord Inhabits the Praises of His People

faith and not by sight. However, I have discovered that even in these learning and stretching times the Lord's presence may still be enjoyed through praise. Last week I was visiting a woman in the hospital who was quite discouraged. She was going through one of those "dark tunnels" in which everything seems hopeless. I began to lead her in a time of praise. Soon the hospital room was filled with a Divine presence. Tears came to her eyes and peace to her soul as God ministered to her. Why don't you pause right now and begin to praise Him? Soon you will be able to "taste and see that the Lord is good" (Ps. 34:8).

23
Praise—The Offensive Weapon

In a very tense moment, the Lord put His disciples on the spot by asking them their conviction regarding His true identity. The first to speak was Peter. "Thou art the Christ, the Son of the living God." Jesus was delighted at Peter's answer. He blessed Peter—not because he had calculated the right answer based on intellect or man's opinion, but because Peter had received this revelation from God the Father.

Jesus then made a very profound statement: Peter, upon your confession, upon the fact that I am the Son of God, I will build my church; and the gates of hell shall not prevail against it.

Have you ever noticed who is on the offensive in this statement? For years I misread this verse and pictured Satan storming the gates of heaven, but with us prevailing! How wrong I was! Upon our confession that Jesus is Lord, we become *offensive* and mount an assault upon the gates of hell; and the defenses of Satan will not withstand our attack.

This total victory was won at Calvary. Christ settled once

for all the major issues of life: Jesus is Lord, Satan is defeated, and the saints of God can reign in power and authority. Indeed, Calvary is the fulcrum of the universe. All earthly and heavenly activity is examined and considered based upon the hours surrounding the death of Jesus. Though Satan thought it was his day of victory, the resurrection insured his ignominious defeat. Any hopes or aspirations Satan was entertaining before the resurrection were obliterated.

But if Satan was rendered powerless, why do we tolerate his activity in our lives? Why do we submit to the oppression he inflicts? In 1 Peter 5:8 we have a good image of Satan's total lack of authority and also of his deceitful intimidation: "Your adversary the devil prowls about like a roaring lion, seeking someone to devour."

Zoologists tell us that only aged lions, those that have lost their quickness and strength, utter a roar when approaching other game. Their only strategy is to frighten their prey with a loud noise to the extent that no resistance is offered. Young lions, to the contrary, are always silent and pursue stealthily. What an appropriate picture of Satan and his strategy. Every action of Satan is merely a bluff! His every move toward a believer is merely a loud roar. He has no power, no legal standing. He has no authority—merely pretense. Yet daily he attacks us. Though he is like an assailant using only a toy gun, he continues to aggressively beseige our lives and systematically interfere with God's plan and design. What can we do to stop him? What has God provided for our defense?

The works of Satan abound in the world today. Homes are being destroyed, children of God are physically ill, emotionally depressed and generally oppressed by the evil

Praise—The Offensive Weapon

one. For too long we have continued to stack up sand bags hoping to repel another assault. We cringe at the thought of another attack from the evil one. We usually have no offensive strategy, just a defensive plan that we hope will be adequate at the time of assault.

It has been pronounced in heaven that the saints overcame the accuser because of two things: one, Christ performed; the other, we must execute.

> And they overcame him because of the blood of the Lamb and because of the word of their testimony (Rev. 12:11).

Christ, by His blood shed on Calvary, "rendered powerless him who had the power of death, that is, the devil." This is the first thing that enables us to overcome: we must remind Satan of the blood which flowed at Calvary. We must supply the second thing mentioned: the word of our testimony. The confession is up to us!

What is the word of our testimony? I believe it is praise: confessing with our lips what Christ has done for us; telling aloud His wonderful character and attributes; exalting Jesus. When Satan attacks, we must confess the truth: Jesus is Lord, Satan is defeated. Our God reigns. Praise the name of Jesus, Hallelujah for the blood, by His stripes we are healed!

By praising God through testimony, we remind Satan of who we are and who he is—and is not. Satan cannot tolerate the praises of God's people because it establishes their authority, links them to the Rock of Ages, elevates them to their heavenly place, and reveals Satan's position of incompetence. Jesus intends for us to actively pursue the enemy and to fight against "the principalities, against the powers, against the world rulers of this present darkness, against the spiritual hosts of wickedness in the heavenly places" (Eph. 6:12). We are not to sit back and try to anticipate his next move; the next move is ours—it is an assault upon the portals of hell!

To execute our offensive attack, we need offensive weapons and a grand strategy to pursue. Both the weapons and the strategy are explained in Psalm 149:

> Praise the Lord! Sing to the Lord a new song . . . Let the godly ones exult in glory; let them sing for joy on their beds. Let the high praises of God be in their mouth, and a two-edged sword in their hand, to execute vengeance on the nations, and punishment on the peoples; to bind their kings [Satan] with chains, and their nobles [demons] with fetters of iron; to execute on them the judgment written. This is an honor for all His godly ones. Praise the Lord!

Two weapons are mentioned in this Psalm. The first is the "high praises of God" in our mouth. We are to sing a new song, we are to exalt in glory and sing for joy. We can use the vocal high praises of God to fight our battle.

The high praises of God are torment to the ears of Satan because they remind him of the heavenly praises in which he participated, and perhaps led. The following passage from Ezekiel implies such a lofty position:

> Thus says the Lord God "You [Lucifier] had the seal of perfection . . . every precious stone was your covering . . . you were the anointed cherub who covers (the throne) . . . you were on

the holy mountain of God; you walked in the midst of stones of fire . . . until unrighteousness was found in you . . . therefore I have cast you as profane from the mountain of God" (Ezek. 28:12-16).

God's praises remind Satan of the heavenly estate he forfeited because of his pride and rebellion. The aural aspect of praising God (and this is why it is important to praise God *out loud)* is a constant reminder of what Satan could be enjoying, and what he will live without in his eternal destiny. As the psalmist tells us, the Lord "inhabits the praises of His people" (Ps. 22:3). Whenever we are aware of Satan's presence, if we begin to praise Jesus, we will soon be aware of another presence—a Holy one. Satan will not abide in the presence of the Lord!

The efforts and works of Satan and his demonic hosts increase in number and intensity as we near the day when the judgment pronounced upon him by God will be executed. Therefore, it becomes increasingly important that God's people learn to use praise as a mighty weapon against the evil host. The evil presence cannot abide very long in the midst of sincere praise uttered from the lips of those who have "clean hands and a pure heart, and have not lifted up their souls to falsehood or sworn deceitfully" (see Ps. 24).

The second weapon mentioned is the "two-edged sword," which Ephesians tells us is the Word of God. How important it is to know the Bible and to be able to use it effectively. And what a powerful combination results when we praise using the Word of God. That is why Scripture choruses are so important and appropriate in worship.

The grand strategy described in Psalm 149 involves binding the strong man and executing on him the judgment which has already been written. We have the privilege to "bind on earth that which has been bound in heaven," and we've only to read the last book of the Bible, Revelation, to discover Satan's end. Heaven has revealed that he will be bound forevermore. Satan is defeated—though he bruised His heel, He crushed his head.

Praise as an offensive weapon should become an integral part of our lives. For too many saints, to speak the name of Jesus aloud is an awkward thing, sometimes embarrassing if overheard. Not only does praise have inherent power, but God is pleased with our outward confession of Him. He endorses our praise with His blessing and power. The name of Jesus should flow freely from our lips, and words telling of His excellence should be a standard part of our vocabulary.

Recall the story of Jehoshaphat, cited in the last chapter. He was King of Judah, and he sought the Lord on behalf of his soon-to-be-invaded country. As all Judah stood before God, Jahaziel, a Levite, was anointed by the Spirit and proclaimed the word of the Lord: "Do not fear or be dismayed because of this great multitude; for the battle is not yours but God's . . . you need not fight this battle . . . for the Lord is with you (2 Chron. 20:15-17).

Jehoshaphat, resting upon this promise, instructed those who sang to the Lord, and those who praised Him in holy attire, to go into battle in front of the army, singing songs of praise. They marched forward as if the battle had already been fought. When they began singing and praising, the Lord set ambushes against the enemy, who were routed. Note the order in which the tribe of Judah went to battle. By sending the musicians first, they were confessing to the Lord and to the enemy their faith in God. They literally praised their way to victory. The world teaches us to be fighters—when the enemy comes, to use our own connivance and strength. God wants us to praise, and, in the act of praise, to rely upon His strength and ability to rout the enemy.

I have seen praise and worship change an entire church. Many times I have walked into an auditorium to begin a song service and immediately felt an oppression. Those present seemed sad, depressed, under a burden, experiencing any number of manifestations of satanic attack. The only successful treatment for this problem seemed to be to lead the people into praise. As we continued to sing and praise, the cloud of oppression was lifted. Instead of beginning praise from a joyful heart, many had to praise themselves into a state of joy. But if we stay with it long enough, the end result of praise is always the same: joy inexpressible and full of glory.

In counseling people who are despondent, often the best advice is to prescribe a daily time of praise, explaining of course that we must praise whether we feel like it or not. It is amazing how often our feelings will come into consonance with what our lips confess. Especially during deliverance sessions, praise is a mighty weapon to combat the work of Satan.

Praise has likewise changed my family. I am teaching my four-year-old daughter to use praise in her life whenever she is afraid, discouraged, or experiencing any other emotion contrary to the Spirit-controlled living. Recently we were in the church building, walking toward my office in the dark, when my daughter hesitated because she thought bad guys might be hiding in the dark. Instead of turning on the light switch, which would have only provided a temporary solution, I spent a minute explaining to her a more powerful, permanent solution. Per my instruction, we continued down the hallway, shouting at the top of our voices, "Jesus, Jesus, Praise the Lord, Hallelujah, Jesus!" As we began to praise Him, we were filled with power, boldness, confidence, assurance, and joy.

Soon after this incident it occurred to me that the lesson was not for children only. What freedom we would experience as adults if, when we became frightened or discouraged, we would praise Him aloud. Some time ago, I talked myself into being discouraged and depressed. That had not happened to me in over four years, but in a matter of two hours, I had convinced myself that circumstances would substantiate my being depressed. I simply confessed out loud all the seemingly negative events from which I could see no deliverance. Satan took me at my word, accepted the authority I had given him, and went to work on me. I moped around for several hours before I realized what had happened. I certainly did not feel like praising the Lord but I *willed* to praise Him. At the time, we lived out in the country and I would often retreat to the front porch for my time of praise. When I began to praise Him, I must admit, my mouth was engaged but my feelings were far removed. But, I believe that such praise is most pleasing to the Lord. It took about twenty minutes, but the Holy Spirit fell, cleansed me of the mire I had fallen into, and raised me up and set me on a rock. Psalm 40 relived! If I had not taken up the weapon of praise and begun to use it, there's no telling how long I would have remained in such a state. I praised my way out of defeat!

Praise—The Offensive Weapon

The next time you sense the deceiver at work, in the life and activity of your family, or in any gathering of the Lord's people, be bold enough to enter praise and observe that as you "resist the devil he will flee from you."

> With the high praises of God in our mouth
> And a two-edged sword in our hand,
> We mount our assault on the portals of hell,
> And against us they shall not stand.
> Singing praise, praise, praise to the Lord,
> Let it ring throughout the land.
> Singing praise, praise, praise to the Lord,
> For the battle is in His hand.
> —Owens

24
Psalms—The Heart of Praise in the Bible

No book on praise would be complete without some type of a discussion, though ever so brief, on the Psalms, which is the longest book in the Bible, and the heart of its praise. The Bible contains numerous passages of well-articulated praise: the Magnificat of Mary (Luke 1:46-55), the Benedictus of Zacharias (Luke 1:68-79), the Gloria of the angels (Luke 2:14), the Nuncdimittis of Simeon (Luke 2:29-32), David's prayer of thanksgiving (1 Chron. 29:10-13), and the Benediction of Jude (Jude 24, 25). But the Psalms contain the most praise Scriptures. Ronald Allen has summarized their significance quite well:

> Only a Philistine could fail to love the Psalms. Of all the books in the Old Testament, the Book of Psalms is the one most loved by the family of God. Within the Psalms we find expression to our deepest thoughts of reverence for God, our most excited joy in knowing Him, and our darkest terror in those moments we feel cut off from Him. In the Psalms we have it all: music, wisdom,

beauty, truth, theology, experience, emotion, and expression. In the Psalms we have the Lord Jesus in bold prophecy and in subtle types. Most of all, in the Psalms we have the praise of God.*

In-depth studies of the Psalms are available in many fine commentaries and exegetical studies. This chapter is intended simply as a catalyst to initiate or rekindle a love and appreciation for the Psalms. They are so infused with human sentiment and experience that one can profit from them even without a technical knowledge of their construction. Herein I offer several observations with the hope that the Psalms may become your primary source book of praise.

The Psalms reveal the praise-life of David.

The Psalms were written by several different authors. Some are ascribed to Asaph (Ps. 73-88; 2 Chron. 29:30); one (Ps. 90) is said to be the prayer of Moses; several are titled "A Psalm of the Sons of Korah" (Ps. 84, 85 and others); and Psalm 137 was obviously penned at the time of the captivity in Babylon. Without question, though, the author of the vast majority of the psalms was David, the son of Jesse, called in 2 Samuel 23 "the sweet psalmist of Israel."

This great king of Israel was not only cunning in battle, he was an artist, a poetic and musical genius. He understood the importance of music and praise and made them integral parts of his life and the life of the nation he ruled. David was the chief praise leader of the Old Testament. We learn the life of faith from Noah and

---
* Ronald Allen, *Praise! A Matter of Life and Breath*, p. 17.

Psalms—The Heart of Praise in the Bible

Abraham, and the life of sanctification from Daniel and Joseph; from the Psalms of David we learn the life of praise.

The Psalms express nearly all human sentiments and provide instruction and consolation for every situation in life.

It is obvious from reading the Psalms that David's song life and praise life were not confined to those occasions when things were going well. David used music to express and strengthen himself at all times. He undoubtedly had learned the value of giving thanks in all things.

When he was being chased by Saul, he sang (Ps. 52, 54); after he had committed adultery with Bathsheba, he chose to express his contrition through music (Ps. 51); when he was sick, he sang a song of praise (Ps. 41); and when he was at his very best, he offered musical praise (Ps. 145). Regardless of our situation, we can always find expression in the Psalms.

When we are discouraged:

O Lord, how my adversaries have increased! Many are rising up against me. Many are saying of my soul, "There is no deliverance for him in God." Arise, O Lord, save me, O my God! For Thou hast smitten all my enemies on the cheek; Thou hast shattered the teeth of the wicked. Salvation belongs to the Lord; Thy blessings be upon Thy people! (Ps. 3:1, 2, 7, 8).

When our prayers seem unanswered:

Answer me when I call, O God of my righteousness! Thou hast relieved me in my distress; be gracious to me and hear my prayer. But know that the Lord has set apart the godly man for Himself; the Lord hears when I call to Him (Ps. 4:1, 3).

When we need mercy in time of trouble:
O Lord, do not rebuke me in Thine anger, nor chasten me in Thy wrath. Be gracious to me, O Lord, for I am pining away; heal me, O Lord, for my bones are dismayed.

Depart from me, all you who do iniquity, for the Lord has heard the voice of my weeping (Ps. 6:1, 2, 8).

When our enemies seem strong:
O Lord my God, in Thee have I taken refuge; save me from all those who pursue me, and deliver me, lest he tear my soul like a lion, dragging me away, while there is none to deliver.
His mischief will return upon his own head, and his violence will descend upon his own pate.
I will give thanks to the Lord according to His righteousness, and will sing praise to the name of the Lord Most High (Ps. 7:1, 2, 16, 17).

When it seems like the Lord has forgotten us:
How long, O Lord? Wilt Thou forget me forever? How long wilt Thou hide Thy face from me?
I will sing to the Lord, because He has dealt bountifully with me (Ps. 13:1, 6).

When we face death:
Preserve me, O God, for I take refuge in Thee.
For Thou wilt not abandon my soul to Sheol, neither wilt Thou allow Thy Holy One to see the pit. Thou wilt

make known to me the path of life; in Thy presence is fulness of joy; in Thy right hand there are pleasures forever (Ps. 16:1, 10, 11).

When we need direction for our lives:
The Lord is my shepherd, I shall not want (Ps. 23:1).

When we fear being overcome:
The Lord is my light and my salvation; whom shall I fear? The Lord is the defense of my life; whom shall I dread? (Ps. 27:1).

When our resources are running out:
O taste and see that the Lord is good; how blessed is the man who takes refuge in Him! O fear the Lord, you His saints; for to those who fear Him, there is no want. The young lions do lack and suffer hunger; but they who seek the Lord shall not be in want of any good thing (Ps. 34:8-10).

When we find it difficult to wait on God:
I waited patiently for the Lord; and He inclined to me, and heard my cry. He brought me up out of the pit of destruction, out of the miry clay; and He set my feet upon a rock making my footsteps firm (Ps. 40:1, 2).

When we have sinned:
Be gracious to me, O God, according to Thy lovingkindness; according to the greatness of Thy compassion blot out my transgressions. Wash me thoroughly from my iniquity, and cleanse me from my sin. For I know my transgressions, and my sin is ever before me (Ps. 51:1-3).

When we are persecuted:

My soul is among lions; I must lie among those who breathe forth fire, even the sons of men, whose teeth are spears and arrows, and their tongue a sharp sword.

My heart is steadfast, O God, my heart is steadfast; I will sing, yes, I will sing praises! (Ps. 57:4, 7).

When we desire to seek God with all our hearts:

O God, Thou art my God; I shall seek Thee earnestly; my soul thirsts for Thee, my flesh yearns for Thee, in a dry and weary land where there is no water. Thus I have beheld Thee in the sanctuary, to see Thy power and Thy glory (Ps. 63:1, 2).

When God has answered our prayers:

Come and hear, all who fear God, and I will tell of what He has done for my soul. I cried to Him with my mouth, and He was extolled with my tongue. But certainly God has heard; He has given heed to the voice of my prayer (Ps. 66:16, 17, 19).

When our hearts are full of praise:

I will extol Thee, my God, O King; and I will bless Thy name forever and ever. Every day I will bless Thee, and I will praise Thy name forever and ever. Great is the Lord, and highly to be praised; and His greatness is unsearchable (Ps. 145:1-3).

The Psalms are a source book for Christian lyrics.

The Psalms were the hymnbook of Israel. They are the actual words sung by David and the children of Israel. The tunes and meters have been forever lost, but the lyrics

Psalms—The Heart of Praise in the Bible

have been preserved. The word "Psalms" is actually a transliteration of the Greek word *psalmoi*, which means "sacred songs sung to musical accompaniment."

Biblical text is always anointed by God (Heb. 4:12; Isa. 40:8, 55:11). What can be more powerful than biblical text set to music? The Psalms were no doubt doubly effective when they were first penned *and* sung. They were not just ordinary lyrics conceived by man, but holy utterances prompted by the Spirit of God, who knew from the beginning that they would become part of the Holy Bible.

Consequently, modern song writers could do no better than to look to the Psalms as a primary source of lyrics. Using Spirit-led creativity, new tunes can be produced which once again allow the Psalms to be sung and accompanied by musical instruments. Indeed, Colossians 3:16 instructs us to use the Psalms to teach and admonish one another. If you want to have a rewarding experience, go off by yourself some day, take out your Bible, and begin singing the Psalms, composing your own melody as you go. (The less musical aptitude you have, the more you might want to seclude yourself!) It will refresh your spirit.

The Psalms are so numbered that if we read five every day, the entire book can be read every month. (Be sure to allow extra time on the 24th day—that is when Psalm 119 occurs.) What a constant source of strength such an endeavour would provide. The Psalms, perhaps more than any other book in the Bible, bear constant reading. Those desiring a life of praise should saturate their souls with the Psalms—memorize them, recite them aloud, sing them, meditate on their truths, and, in so doing, capture the essence of their message. Praise to the Lord!

25
The Fruit of Our Lips

The Bible has a lot to say about the power of the tongue. Though it is a small member of the body, it is very powerful and in many ways controls the destiny of an individual. Indeed, James 3 says that a man may consider himself perfect if he can totally control his tongue. It is so powerful primarily because what we say, that is, speak aloud, is a direct statement of our will. God, the devil, and anyone else who hears accept what we say as our decision regarding any given situation. The implication here is so great that even if our minds are not totally settled on a decision, if we speak an answer, that becomes our position. Our mind can be thinking one thing, but if our mouth proclaims something different, then what we have said, not what we are thinking, is recorded as our decision.

When we encounter unfortunate circumstances or find ourselves in a dire predicament, we have a decision to make. Are we going to praise the Lord and rejoice in all things, or are we going to be depressed and let the circumstances get us down? Suppose that while contemplating the decision, we happen to enter a conversation with a friend and begin to tell about our ill fate, and, almost without thinking, remark, "I'm depressed about the situation. I don't think it will ever end!" Though we may not totally believe that, nevertheless, our mouth has committed our volition to that stance. The devil is now set free to use that depression to make matters worse, and the Lord, not willing to go against our will, is restricted. If, however, we respond by saying, "Jesus is Lord and He is in control of my circumstances. I choose to praise Him," then God is free to work in our midst and Satan is deprived of a foothold. We must be careful what we say!

Our mouth is either an asset or a liability. If we have the tendency to talk too much, we should study James 1:19. It is always appropriate to utter the praises of God. Indeed, our lips were created that they might confess the excellencies of the Creator. Nothing we can say is more suitable than words of adoration to the Trinity.

Hebrews 13:15 says, "Through Him then, let us continually offer up a sacrifice of praise to God, that is, the fruit of lips that give thanks to His name." My heart's desire is that I would train my lips to give thanks to His name. The fruit of such speaking, that is, the result of giving thanks to His name, is praise.

We had better learn how to express ourselves to God; it is often the only thing that keeps us from spiritually bursting with the glory of God. Revelation 5 records an interesting scene: At least one hundred million angels, beasts, and elders are around the throne saying with a loud voice, "Worthy is the Lamb that was slain . . ." Why are they shouting? Is God hard of hearing? Are these numbers so small that they must be loud to be heard? No! They are shouting because they are before

The Fruit of Our Lips

the throne, because their hearts and spirits are full to bursting!

In our love for God, we will be worse off suppressing our emotions than releasing them. We need words to say and songs to sing; that is why we must develop the fruit of our lips.

People often ask me, "What do you say when you praise the Lord? I usually run out of words and phrases after a minute or two has passed." I too found myself in that same predicament when I first began to make vocal praise a regular part of my life. What *do* you say? Although repetition is not bad, how do you maintain thirty or forty minutes of praise without extreme redundancy?

It is not unusual to be confronted with the challenge of learning a new vocabulary. I recently began using a computer in my office for word processing and file management. I spent several days studying the instruction manuals and became frustrated because the manuals were written in a language that I was unaccustomed to reading. To function properly in that discipline, I had to learn a new vocabulary. I would experience the same deficiency upon entering any unfamiliar field. So why do we find it strange that we must learn the vocabulary of praise?

Praise is the language of heaven! In heaven, the inhabitants do not discuss the weather, nor talk about sports; they are consumed by one passion—expressing to Jesus His worthiness. I am afraid that when many saints get to heaven, they will be in the same predicament I would be in if I took the wrong airline flight and ended up in New Delhi—speechless due to unfamiliarity with the langauge. It is time we became fluent in the heavenly language.

We have at our disposal a vast amount of written material which has as its content and purpose the praise of God. I call this literature "manuscripts of praise." Sometimes these manuscripts can be found as lyrics in an old hymnbook, sometimes as the writing on the walls of an old cathedral, or in the recorded prayers of a contemporary author. If you look for them, you can find them everywhere. These "manuscripts of praise" have several things in common. They are always addressed to God, and they always maintain the integrity and majesty of God, usually avoiding colloquial expressions. I usually keep a good supply of these "manuscripts of praise" in my Bible so I will have them to use when needed. Many phrases should be committed to memory. I often have people repeat them after me, one line at a time. They make excellent material for family devotions, performed responsively. It is good to start the day by voicing this literature of praise.

I have listed a few of these manuscripts on the following pages. Included are several passages of Scripture, which are always doubly effective because they are God's Word. Obviously, the entire book of Psalms could be included. I encourage you to begin your own collection, and make it a regular practice to speak them aloud. The fruit of your lips, instead of being contaminated, will be recognized as praise, honorable and pleasing to the Lord.

Manuscripts of Praise

Te Deum

The authorship of the *Te Deum* is uncertain, though tradition relates that when St. Ambrose baptized St. Augustine in 387 A.D., they spontaneously improvised it in alternate Latin verses. An English translation follows:

The Fruit of Our Lips

We praise Thee, O God, we acknowledge
 Thee to be the Lord.
All the earth doth worship Thee, the Father everlasting.
To Thee all Angels cry aloud; the Heavens, and all the Powers therein;
To Thee Cherubim and Seraphim continually do cry.
Holy, Holy, Holy, Lord God of Sabaoth;
Heaven and earth are full of the Majesty of Thy glory.
The glorious company of the Apostles praise thee.
The goodly fellowship of the Prophets praise Thee.
The noble army of Martyrs praise Thee.
The holy Church throughout all the world doth acknowledge Thee:
The Father, of an infinite Majesty;
Thine adorable, true, and only Son;
Also the Holy Ghost, the Comforter.

Thou art the King of Glory, O Christ.
Thou art the everlasting Son of the Father.
When Thou tookest upon Thee to deliver man,
 Thou didst humble Thyself to be born of a Virgin.
When Thou hadst overcome the sharpness of death,
 Thou didst open the Kingdom of Heaven to all believers.
 Thou sittest at the right hand of God,
 in the glory of the Father,
We believe that Thou shall come to be our Judge.
We therefore pray Thee, help Thy servants, whom Thou
 has redeemed with Thy precious blood.
Make them to be numbered with Thy Saints,
 in glory everlasting.
O Lord, save Thy people, and bless Thine heritage.
Govern them, and lift them up for ever.

Day by day we magnify Thee;
And we worship Thy name forever, world without end.
Vouchsafe, O Lord, to keep us this day without sin.
O Lord, have mercy upon us, have mercy upon us.
O Lord, let Thy mercy be upon us, as our trust is in Thee.
O Lord, in Thee have I trusted;
　let me never be confounded.

Jude 24:25

Now to Him who is able to keep you from stumbling, and to make you stand in the presence of His glory blameless with great joy, to the only God our Savior, through Jesus Christ our Lord, be glory, majesty, dominion and authority, before all time and now and forever. Amen.

1 Chronicles 29:10-13

So David blessed the Lord in the sight of all the assembly; and David said, "Blessed art Thou, O Lord God of Israel our father, forever and ever. Thine, O Lord, is the greatness and the power and the glory and the victory and the majesty, indeed everything that is in the heavens and the earth; Thine is the dominion, O Lord, and Thou dost exalt Thyself as head over all. Both riches and honor come from Thee, and Thou dost rule over all, and in Thy hand is power and might; and it lies in Thy hand to make great, and to strengthen everyone. Now therefore, our God, we thank Thee, and praise Thy glorious name.

Praise the Lord! Ye Heavens, Adore Him

>Praise the Lord, ye heavens, adore Him;
>Praise Him, angels, in the height;
>Sun and moon, rejoice before Him;
>Praise Him, all ye stars of light.
>Praise the Lord! for He hath spoken;
>Worlds His mighty voice obeyed;
>Law which never shall be broken
>For their guidance hath He made.
>
>Praise the Lord! for He is glorious;
>Never shall His promise fail;
>God hath made His saints victorious;
>Sin and death shall not prevail.
>Praise the God of our salvation!
>Hosts on high, His power proclaim;
>Heaven and earth and all creation
>Laud and magnify His name. Amen.

Prayer of Worship (Murchison)

Father, we cast ourselves at your feet. You are the Lord God Almighty, Who keeps covenant from everlasting to everlasting. We acknowledge You as the God above all gods. You are exalted above all the heavens and the earth. There is no one like You, Lord. You are King, God!!! Supreme in your authority. Unquestionable in your sovereignty. Majestic in your splendor. Unparalleled in your greatness. Limitless in your power. Infinite in your wisdom and your knowledge. Absolute in your justice. Magnificent in your splendor. Dazzling in your beauty. Ingenious in your creativity. Timeless in your existence. Terrible in your wrath. Unsearchable in your understanding. Indescribable in your tenderness.

Unfathomable in your love. Matchless in your grace. Unswerving in your faithfulness. Unending in your mercy. Blazing in your glory. Awesome in your holiness. Pristine in your purity. Fascinating in your personality. God!!! God!!! God!!! O, how our hearts leap within us as we look at You and say, "O for grace to love You more.*

Jesus, the Very Thought of Thee
(Bernard of Clairvaux)

Jesus, the very thought of Thee with sweetness fills my breast;
But sweeter far Thy face to see, and in Thy presence rest.
No voice can sing, nor heart can frame, nor can the mem'ry find
A sweeter sound than Thy blest name, O Saviour of mankind.
O Hope of ev'ry contrite heart, O Joy of all the meek,
To those who fall, how kind Thou art! How good to those who seek!
But what to those who find? Ah, this, no tongue nor pen can show;
The love of Jesus, what it is none but His loved ones know.
Jesus, our only joy be Thou, as Thou our prize shalt be;
Jesus, be Thou our glory now, and thro' eternity. Amen.

Prayer of Thanksgiving

O Lord our God, the Author and Giver of all good things; We thank Thee for all thy mercies, and for Thy lovingcare over all Thy creatures. We bless Thee for the gift of life; for Thy protection round about us; for Thy guiding hand upon us; And for all the tokens of Thy love. We thank Thee for friendship and duty; for good hopes and precious memories; for the joys that cheer us; and the trials that teach us to trust in Thee. Most of all we thank Thee for the saving knowledge of Thy Son our Saviour; for the living presence of Thy Spirit, the Comforter; for Thy Church, the Body of Christ; for the ministry of the Word; for the means of grace; and for the hope of glory. In all these things, O Heavenly Father, make us wise unto a right use of Thy benefits; that we may render an acceptable thanksgiving unto Thee all the days of our life; through Jesus Christ our Lord.*

Worship (anonymous)

>Honor and glory, power and salvation
>Be in the highest unto Him who reigneth.
>Changeless in heaven, over earthly changes,
>God, the eternal.
>
>Bow down before Him, people and nations,
>See ye His glory, clearly now appearing.
>Come ye and worship Him, God in the highest,
>Ruler for ever. Amen.

Worship (William Kethe)

>All people that on earth do dwell,
>Sing to the Lord with cheerful voice.
>Him serve with mirth, His praise forth tell;
>Come ye before Him and rejoice.
>
>Know that the Lord is God indeed;
>Without our aid He did us make;
>We are His folk, He doth us feed,
>And for His sheep He doth us take.

---

* *The Hymnbook*, published by Presbyterian Church, p. 10, 11.

O enter then His gates with praise,
Approach with Joy His courts unto;
Praise, laud, and bless His Name always,
For it is seemly so to do.

For why, the Lord our God is good;
His mercy is for ever sure;
His truth at all times firmly stood,
And shall from age to age endure. Amen.

General Hymn (Richard Mant, 1824)

God, my King, thy might confessing,
Ever will I bless thy Name;
Day by day thy throne addressing,
Still will I thy praise proclaim.

Honor great our God befitteth;
Who his majesty can reach?
Age to age his works transmitteth,
Age to age his power shall teach.

They shall talk of all thy glory,
On thy might and greatness dwell,
Speak of thy dread acts the story,
And thy deeds of wonder tell.

Nor shall fail from memory's treasure
Works by love and mercy wrought,
Works of love surpassing measure,
Works of mercy passing thought.

Full of kindness and compassion,
Slow to anger, vast in love,
God is good to all creation;
And his works his goodness prove.

All thy works, O Lord, shall bless thee;
Thee shall all thy saints adore:
King supreme shall they confess thee,
And proclaim thy sovereign power. Amen.

General Hymn (Johann Mentzer, 1704)
O that I had a thousand voices,
  A thousand ways to praise my God!
In him my inmost heart rejoices
  Until I long to tell abroad
In songs of thankful ecstasy
How much my God hath done for me.

Who overwhelmeth me with blessing?
  Who but thyself, O God of love!
Who guardeth me from fears oppressing?
  'Tis thou, Lord God of hosts, above.
Thou bearest all my guilt abhorred,
With ever patient mercy, Lord.

Thy goodness, Lord, my life completeth;
  O let thy praise my tongue employ,
And bring to thee, while my heart yet beateth,
  The glad thanksgiving of my joy:
When ebbing strength all speech denies,
Then may I breathe thy praise in sighs.

My God, receive these earthly praises
  So poor and weak, with gracious love;
A better tribute heaven raises
  From all thy angels choirs above:
There alleluias will I bring
A thousand-fold to thee, my King. Amen.

General Hymn (F.W. Faber)

My God, how wonderful Thou art,
    Thy majesty how bright,
How beautiful Thy mercy-seat,
    In depths of burning light!

How dread are Thine eternal years,
    O everlasting Lord,
By prostrate spirits day and night
    Incessantly adored!

How wonderful, how beautiful,
    The sight of Thee must be,
Thine endless wisdom, boundless power,
    And awful purity!

Oh, how I fear Thee, Living God,
    With deepest, tenderest fears,
And worship Thee with trembling hope,
    And penitential tears!

Yet I may love Thee too, O Lord,
    Almighty as Thou art,
For Thou hast stoop'd to ask of me
    The love of my poor heart.

No earthly father loves like Thee,
    No mother, e'er so mild,
Bears and forbears as Thou hast done
    With me Thy sinful child.

Father of Jesus, love's reward,
    What rapture will it be,
Prostrate before Thy Throne to lie,
    And gaze and gaze on Thee.

26
The Vocabulary of Praise

Numerous words and phrases in the Bible make up the vocabulary of praise. They are used quite often in our praise language and are naturally well-suited for expressing our thoughts to God. They occur frequently throughout the Bible, particularly in the Psalms. Unfortunately, for many, they have been spoken so many times that they have become cliches. It is also possible that some have never really understood the correct meaning of a word or phrase, and therefore have used it without understanding its significance.

In an attempt to eliminate these pitfalls, and with the hope of heightening our praise experience, some of the most notable expressions are herein defined and discussed. I want to especially acknowledge Dr. Ronald Allen and his excellent book, *Praise! A Matter of Life and Breath.** Dr. Allen has given insight into the Hebrew meaning of many of the words listed below.

---

* Ronald Allen, *Praise! A Matter of Life and Breath* (Nashville: Thomas Nelson, 1980).

Praise

Halah (Hebrew): To be clear, to make a show, to boast, to celebrate, to shine (Ps. 113:1; 2 Chron. 29:30).

Halah is an ecstatic shout of joy. It is the extemporaneous, unsolicited response to a favorable and joyful situation. It is the reaction one has when his favorite football team has just scored the winning points. When we *halal* the Lord, we "make clear" His glory; we "boast" of Him; we "rave" over Him; we "shine" upon Him and magnify Him.

A familiar term often used in praise is "Hallelujah." It is simply a transliteration of the Hebrew word *halal* and as such means "praise the Lord."

> And they are to stand every morning to thank
> and to praise the Lord, and likewise at evening
> (1 Chron. 23:30).

Epainos, ainos (Greek): overflowing, joyful praise (Eph. 1:5-6).

When the word "praise" occurs in the New Testament, it is most often a translation of one of these words. As in the Hebrew *halal*, the feeling is one of overflowing, joyful expression. Do you remember how you felt when you passed that big exam? Do you recall what you said and how you expressed yourself? Similiar feelings are expressed by these words.

> . . . having been filled with the fruit of right-
> eousness which comes through Jesus Christ, to
> the glory and praise of God (Phil. 1:11).

Bless

Barak (Hebrew): to kneel, to bless God (Ps. 103:2).

This is an interesting word whose meaning may not be

The Vocabulary of Praise

initially obvious. We can think of blessing from two different perspectives, our blessing God, and God blessing us.

What exactly are we asking when we ask God to "bless" the food before we partake, or when we ask Him to "bless" an offering, or a program we intend to begin? When God blesses something, He allows it to be, or do, or accomplish more than it normally would without His blessing. When we pray, "Lord, bless this offering of $300," we are asking Him to allow that amount of money to do more than what $300 could do under ordinary circumstances. When we ask the Lord to bless a program, we are expecting Him to supernaturally multiply our investment of time, money, and energy toward a more profitable outcome.

If this is the meaning of God blessing something, what does it mean for us to bless God? Surely we cannot hope to add to Him who is all and all. An understanding of parallelism in Hebrew writing gives us a source of understanding. Allen explains parallelism in this way:

> "Parallelism is one statement followed by another, done with art, style, and image. By saying the same thing in slightly different words, the total impression is enhanced beyond saying either line alone."*

In essence, parallelism is saying the same thing twice, using different terms. Its purpose is to enhance meaning. Psalm 103:2 helps us understand the term "bless" as it applies to our praise of God: "Bless the Lord, O my soul, And forget none of His benefits."

This is an example of antithetical parallelism in which the

---

* Ronald Allen, *Praise! A Matter of Life and Breath*, p. 51.

first line is enhanced by the denial of its opposite. The opposite of blessing the Lord is to forget His benefits. Therefore, blessing the Lord involves recalling and enumerating all of His acts of love toward us. Do you wish to bless the Lord? Proclaim aloud (which is parallelism from Ps. 66:8) the faithfulness of the Lord; remember His acts of compassion; recall the good and perfect gifts He has bestowed! What an honorable way to praise the Lord.

> Bless our God, O peoples,
> And sound His praise abroad
> (Ps. 66:8).

Eulogeo (Greek): *eu:* well, good, well done; *logos:* something said, word (Luke 2:28).

To bless in the New Testament, therefore, means to speak well of, to praise, to acknowledge His goodness.

> With it (the tongue) we bless our Lord and Father (James 3:9).

Sing

Shuwr (Hebrew): to sing.
> Sing to the Lord a new song;
> Sing to the Lord, all the earth (Ps. 96:1).

Zamar (Hebrew): to strike with the fingers, to touch the parts of a musical instrument, to make music, to sing forth praise.

> So I will sing praise to Thy name forever (Ps. 61:8).

Ranan (Hebrew): to shout, rejoice, cry out.
> O come, let us sing for joy to the Lord; Let us shout joyfully to the rock of our salvation (Ps. 95:1).

The Vocabulary of Praise

Music played a prominent role in the life and worship of the Old Testament saints. The Old Testament refers to singing no less than 172 times. It was not an extra-curricular activity; it was an integral part of the worship which was at the very center of Hebrew life.

Their singing must have been scintillating. Though the actual sounds are lost forever, the music must have been grand, and probably very professionally rendered, since the Levites were solely devoted to that task. Imagine yourself in the midst of this praise gathering:

> And all the Levitical singers, Asaph, Heman, Jeduthun, and their sons and kinsmen, clothed in fine linen, with cymbals, harps, and lyres, standing east of the altar, and with them one hundred and twenty priests blowing trumpets, in unison when the trumpeters and the singers were to make themselves heard with one voice to praise and to glorify the Lord, and when they lifted up their voice accompanied by trumpets and cymbals and instruments of music, and when they praised the Lord saying, "He indeed is good for His lovingkindness is everlasting," then the house, the house of the Lord, was filled with a cloud, so that the priests could not stand to minister because of the cloud, for the glory of the Lord filled the house of God (2 Chron. 5:12-14).

Ado (Greek): to praise (Eph. 5:19; Rev. 5:9).

This verb is always used in reference to praise of God.

> Let the word of Christ richly dwell within you; with all wisdom teaching and admonishing one another with psalms and hymns and spiritual songs, singing with thankfulness in your hearts to God (Col. 3:16).

Psallo (Greek): originally, playing a stringed instrument with the fingers, perhaps a harp; In New Testmament usage, to sing, or to sing a hymn of praise (1 Cor. 14:15).

> Is anyone cheeful? Let him sing praises (James 5:13).

Humneo (Greek): the noun form, *humnos,* denotes a song of praise addressed to God; the verb form implies the singing of a hymn (Acts 16:25).

> And after singing a hymn, they went out to the Mount of Olives (Matt. 26:30).

In modern worship, the most effective means of praise is music and, in particular, singing. Music has a special way of linking our spirits with the Spirit of God. When singing God-honoring lyrics, we greatly enhance the communication process. I once read a sign quoting Augustine which said, "He who sings, prays twice." The syntax is a little confusing in this phrase, but the thought is a good one.

A good barometer of the life of a church is its congregational singing. When people are filled with the joy of the Lord, they forget that they "can't sing" and begin to try. The result, I'm sure, pleases the Lord.

Shout

Ranan (Hebrew): to shout for joy, cry out, be joyful (Ps. 132:9).

> . . . and shout for joy all you who are upright in heart (Ps. 32:11).

Ruwa (Hebrew): to split the ears with sound, to shout, make a joyful noise (2 Chron. 13:15).

> O clap your hand, all peoples; shout to God with the voice of joy (Ps. 47:1).

The Vocabulary of Praise

As we read the Psalms and other accounts of worship among the Hebrews, we soon realize that Old Testament worship was basically loud in nature. This was especially true in corporate worship. Though I'm sure David played many soft melodies on his harp, when it came to celebrating the goodness of God among the people, the Hebrew praise was vivacious, exuberant, high-sounding, and powerful.

As a musician, I would be the first to admit that loud is not better than soft. Dynamics, a variable of music, is used to enhance the total effect of what is being communicated. Hence, it becomes a matter of appropriateness. When we gather in corporate worship to celebrate the greatness of God, is it more appropriate to be loud or soft? Obviously, every situation will determine the answer to that question, but experience leads me to believe that it will usually lean toward higher decibel level.

That leads us to the word under observation—"to shout." There's no way to shout softly. Scripture is teaching here that shouts to God are a good and acceptable manner of praise. During the Jesus movement of the early 70's, many were offended by "Jesus yells." Though the practice was new to this age, it was not new to God's Kingdom and perhaps was just a regeneration of an old and forgotten method of praise. Of course, every outward spiritual expression must come from a sincere heart and, and the more obvious the expression, the great the need for sincerity. If one is going to shout to God, he must be sure his motives are pure; otherwise the attention drawn to the flesh would nullify any spiritual gain.

Thank
Yadah (Hebrew): literally to hold out the hand, to revere or

worship with extended hands, to make confession, to give thanks (Neh. 12:24; Ps. 105:1, 107:1).

In most English translations of the Bible, the Hebrew word *yadah* is rendered "to thank." There is some reservation among scholars as to this translation; some even say there is no Hebrew word meaning "to thank." Indeed, by observing the above literal meanings, the word takes on a different thought. Inherent in the expression is the desire to publicly acknowledge the Lord and to tell of His great works. The term implies a vocal, forthright statement of our love and devotion to God.

> Therefore I will give thanks to Thee, O Lord, among the nations, and I will sing praises to Thy name (2 Sam. 22:50).

Eucharisteo (Greek): to be grateful, to express gratitude, to use grateful language (Col. 1:12; Rev. 11:17).

Unlike *yadah,* the Greek word *eucharisteo* is very much akin to the English concept of giving thanks. Christian people must be noted for possessing a grateful spirit, especially toward the Lord. Ingratitude surfaces only in the heart of one who is either incognizant of the goodness of the Lord, or one who knows the Lord's goodness but is so consumed by self that he sees no need to show appreciation. Giving thanks to God is only natural and as such it is an integral part of praise.

> And having said this, he took bread and gave thanks to God in the presence of all; and he broke it and began to eat (Acts 27:35).

Magnify
Gadal (Hebrew): to make large, advance, boast, increase,

The Vocabulary of Praise

lift up, promote, proudly speak of (Pss. 35:27, 69:30; 1 Chron. 17:24).

God is all in all, and, as such, He cannot be added to or made larger; His glory cannot be increased, and His character cannot be altered by anything we may or may not do. What then does it mean, to magnify the Lord? When used in reference to God, magnify means to speak well of, or to lift up and promote. It is merely to hold in high esteem or to boast of that which already exists. When we magnify God, we simply admire and brag on who He is and what He has done. It is similar in action to enlarging a photograph; the subject matter does not change but the presentation is heightened. It is like the awesomeness which comes from reading a book on astronomy after having only viewed the sky with the naked eye, having not understood its vastness and intricacy.

When we expound on the character and attributes of God, we are magnifying Him; when we testify of His faithfulness in our lives, we do the same; our expressions of gratitude for His goodness and mercy are also ways of magnifying the Lord. The old-time "testifying meetings" were fulfillments of this scriptural command.

> O magnify the Lord with me, and let us exalt His name together (Ps. 34:3).

Megaluno (Greek): to make great, enlarge, show as great (Acts 10:46).

Mary, the mother of Jesus, upon receiving yet another confirmation that she was to bear the Son of God, responded by exalting her Lord.

> My soul doth magnify the Lord, and my spirit hath rejoiced in God my Saviour (Luke 1:46-47 KJV).

Those advanced in the understanding of God's grace and mercy, like Mary, are those who think the most highly of God, and desire to express that. There are those who would say, "Who is the Almighty, that we should serve Him?" (Job 21:15), because they have never tasted the goodness of the Lord. The more honor God gives a man the more he should study to magnify Him.

It is frequently much too easy to identify, define, study, and discuss terminology. We should now have a better understanding of these terms, but knowledge should motivate us to action. It is of little value to read about praise if we never engage in the act. Why not pause for a moment right now and magnify the Lord!

27
Rocks, Be Silent!

I am writing this chapter in the midst of a mission tour in the north-western U.S. and Canada. We have been privileged to see some of the most beautiful handiwork of God's creation. We went to the base of Mount Rainier yesterday. It was one of those unusually clear days in Washington State and the beautiful snow-covered mountain was etched into the background of cloudless blue sky. The sight was breath-taking to say the least, and it caused something to swell up within me, something so compelling that I would have had to sin to keep it inside; my heart was full of adoration and praise. In the evening, the mountain prevailed against a star-spangled sky and once again the urge was overwhelming. A ferry ride across Puget Sound provided the same inspiration as did the multitude of beautiful flowers displayed in the Butchart Gardens.

There are times in life when praise seems the only appropriate thing to do, when there is such a manifestation of God's greatness and glory that to refrain from praise would be to quench the spirit of God, and to miss a good opportunity to restore the soul. During these times, praise is a very natural thing; to abstain is unnatural to our spirit.

Entering His Presence

It most often happens in a natural setting in which God's creation is displayed, but, then again, it could strike just about anywhere. I remember my wife and I walking into an Episcopal cathedral in Washington, D.C. The architecture and decor were magnificent, the sun was penetrating the multi-colored stained glass windows, and a holy presence was felt. I immediately sensed that this was one of those times. I had the time of my life singing several stanzas of "Holy, Holy, Holy" a cappella, as loud as I could. It was as if praise, in that instant, was demanded; all created forces were prepared to sympathetically respond and be released through the sounds of praise.

God gives us these special times in which praise is at a premium, in which it is not only easy to praise the Lord but the occasion almost demands it. Having benefited from many of these experiences, I have become accustomed to looking for these, seeking them out, even praying for them. They are times of refreshment, encouragment, and sublime communion.

I've already said that praise should be an unceasing activity in our lives. We should praise Him in the good times and the bad, when we feel like it and when we do not, when our hearts are sorrowful and when they are full of joy. This consistent praise life is necessary and most honoring to God; but praise God as well for those time's when praise comes easy, when we can almost feel His presence, and when the desire to praise is predominant. In faith, we praise Him when the circumstances are discouraging, but what a double joy to praise Him when the circumstances are liberating!

The Bible records such an occasion in Luke 19:37-40:

Rocks, Be Silent!

And as He was now approaching, near the descent of the Mount of Olives, the whole multitude of the disciples began to praise God joyfully with a loud voice for all the miracles which they had seen, saying, "Blessed is the King who comes in the Name of the Lord; peace in heaven and glory in the highest!"

And some of the Pharisees in the multitude said to Him, "Teacher, rebuke Your disciples."

And He answered and said, "I tell you, if these become silent, the stones will cry out!"

When Christ was making His triumphal entry into Jerusalem, the people were giving Him praise; it was a grand event. He who had lived and ministered in such a humble and unpretentious manner was finally allowing a little pomp and circumstance. Although it was far from the type of processional the King of kings deserved, there was a certain amount of grandeur involved.

If there was ever a time to praise Jesus during His earthly ministry, it was then. Many of the disciples began to laud Him, but ironically, some of the religious leaders began to feel uncomfortable with all the loud praise and attempted to quiet the children. The Lord reprimanded them sharply. He said, "If these children cease praising me, the stones which surround us will immediately cry out!" What an indictment against those who do not praise. The Lord in essence said, "If you, who were created in my image and for whom I will give my life, refuse to praise me, then these inanimate rocks will. If you will not do that which should be natural to you, the rocks will have to do that which is unnatural to them." There is a great lesson to be learned from this incident. *The Lord will be praised.* His name and holiness will not be without proper acknowledgment. The Lord is most honored by our intelligent, volitional praise, but if this is found lacking, God's creation will stand in the gap.

Have the rocks ever had to cry out on your behalf? Have you ever been so busy or insensitive that the Lord had to go to "Plan Two" in order to receive the glory He desired and deserved? Has your pride ever kept you from entering spontaneous worship? I recall with much sorrow a time in my life when I refrained when I should have rejoiced. Our five-year-old daughter had been given a hearing test and it was discovered that she only had 50% hearing in her left ear. For three weeks I prayed into that ear, I praised into that ear, and I confessed the healing power of Jesus in that ear. When we returned to the ear specialist for more advanced tests, the results showed that she had perfect hearing in both ears. God had healed her ear! My heart leapt in gratitude to God, but my tongue remained silent. I suppose I was intimidated by the austerity of the doctor's office. I do not know what God had to use in that office to applaud Him, maybe a chair or a stethescope, but I am quite sure He was praised. I had lost forever a good opportunity to testify of the greatness of my Lord.

If we do not worship the Lord, it is not He who will be without, it is us. All through the Bible, when saints have seen a glimpse of heaven they have always seen and heard the incessant praise of God. God's throne has always been, is now, and will forever be surrounded and enshrined with pure praise. Our praise does not increase His glory nor does our lack of praise decrease His magnificence. He alone is worthy to be praised, and the very concept and act of praise was created by God and exclusively for God.

Back to the incident in Luke 19. This was one of those occasions when praise was a must; the situation demanded it! Jesus had just performed many miracles before their eyes, and there was majestic sweetness enthroned upon His head. The Bible says there is a time for all things (Eccles. 3:1), a time to be cheerful and a time to consider sorrow (James 5:13). The appropriate action at this time was praise! It was not a time to pray for the sick; it was a time to praise!

You may say, "I never seem to have these special occasions. God does not favor me by providing these unique praise opportunities." If all else is well (i.e., your sin is confessed up to date, you are yielded to the Spirit, etc.), there are two possible reasons why God may withhold such encounters. First, the Bible says that those who seek the Lord shall surely find Him (Jer. 29:13). The implication is that if we do not seek God, we will probably not find Him. Does your soul long for such communion? Do you pray for it? Do you anticipate those special times of worship? If you do not, you will probably never enjoy them.

Second, the Lord is more apt to reveal himself to those whom He knows will worship Him. I have a friend who is always leading people to Jesus. It seems as if God is always bringing people across his path who are ready and willing to be saved. I once asked him why this is so. His simple response was, "Because the Lord knows that I will be faithful to witness. He trusts me." That makes a lot of sense! God leads ripe fruit his way because He knows he is a skilled harvester and will be faithful to harvest. Could it be that God allows His glory to be seen by men whom He knows will praise Him? If God knows there is worship in your heart, He will give you good reason to express it.

Rocks, be silent! We will be sensitive to recognize those times when praise is demanded—and we will praise. We will anticipate those special times and no matter where we are or who is around, we will praise Him aloud. We will not be intimidated by those who may see or those who may criticize. Our heart's cry is:

> Be silent ye mountains, ye hills and ye fountains, for this is the time I must sing. It's the time to sing praises to the rock of all ages, and this is the time I must sing.
>
> Gaither

28
Lessons From the Tabernacle

Many Christians testify that a study of the tabernacle and its related meanings and symbolisms can be one of the most life-changing events in a person's life. It is a study of nearly inexhaustible depth and provides a good spiritual nourishment for all saints no matter where they are in their walk with the Lord. Within its teachings, we find insight into almost every major biblical theme. Worship is no exception. As a matter of fact, Exodus 25 tells us that communion was the primary purpose of the tabernacle: "And let them construct a sanctuary for Me, *that I may dwell among them*" (v. 8, emphasis added). Our understanding of the art of worship will be greatly enhanced by a brief study of the tabernacle and its object lessons.

The tabernacle served as the center of Jewish worship for nearly 500 years, from Moses to David, until it was replaced by a permanent structure, the Temple, during the reign of Solomon. The design of the edifice, its furniture, utensils, even the materials used in its construction, all gave evidence of God's plan of providing man with a means of coming into His presence. It was and still is a master lesson on how we can go about approaching the throne of God.

The tabernacle consisted of three main areas: the Outer Court, the Holy Place, and the Holy of Holies. God's presence resided in the Holy of Holies. The process of getting there was explicitly outlined by God and was completely followed by any priest who hoped to succeed in the course.

Entering the presence of God involved many steps. Upon entering the eastern gate, the priest came into a large open-air outer court. The area, 150 by 75 feet, was outlined by long, white curtains seven feet tall. The outer court was exposed to all the elements and could be seen by all. Within this outer court, the priest would encounter two articles of furniture: the brazen altar and the brazen laver. The altar, in the form of a hollow box, was where the priest would offer both gifts and sacrifices for sins (Heb. 5:1). The sin offering and the trespass offering made atonement for those on whose behalf they were presented. Here the priest would offer the blood of animals for the sins of the people. Dedicatory offerings (meal offerings, peace offerings), were acts of total consecration, their purpose being to present a life wholly devoted to God.

At the laver of water, the priests were to wash their hands and feet of any impurity before handling the vessels of the Lord. Their instruction was, "And Aaron and his sons shall wash their hands and their feet from it; when they enter the tent of meeting, they shall wash with water, that they may not die" (Exod. 30:20, 21). The washing at the laver represented a cleansing that was necessary for any spiritual duty. If the altar was the place for reconciliation, the laver was the source of sanctification.

Lessons From the Tabernacle

The Holy Place was a tent, covered on top and on all sides. Situated in the rear of the courtyard, it measured 45 feet long by 15 feet wide. Within this tent were three articles of furniture: the golden candlestick, the table of shewbread, and the golden altar of incense.

The seven-light candlestick provided the only source of light, for there were no windows in the tent of meeting. It was to burn continually (Lev. 24:2) to give the necessary light for the priests to carry out their duties.

The table of shewbread was to always contain twelve loaves of holy bread. It was a very high-quality bread made from fine flour. The priests were to eat the twelve loaves (one for each tribe) as God's representatives of the nation. The immediate purpose of the table of shewbread was to provide food and fellowship for God's priests.

The third article of furniture in the Holy Place was the altar of incense, which was positioned directly in front of the veil leading to the Holy of Holies. Upon the altar the priests would burn a specially compounded incense (Exod. 30) every morning and at evening time. The ministry here was one of adoration and intercession. The sweet fragrance emitted by the incense was a fragrance to God representing the praise and prayers of the people.

The back one-third of the tent of meeting was set off by a veil which hung from the roof to the floor. Behind the veil was the Holy of Holies, and within it was the ark of the covenant and the mercy seat. Whereas the Holy Place was entered daily by the ministering priests, the Holy of Holies was entered only once a year, and then only by the high priest. It was within this chamber that God focused His presence; it was His throne room.

The ark of the covenant contained Aaron's rod that budded, manna from the wilderness, and the two tablets of the covenant given to Moses (Heb. 9:4). The mercy seat was the throne of the tabernacle. It was there that God said,"And there I will meet with thee, and I will commune with thee from above the mercy seat" (Exod. 25:22 KJV). Every year on the Day of Atonement the high priest would sprinkle the blood of the propitiation on the mercy seat. Because of the all-sufficiency of Christ, represented by the ark of the covenant, and the mercy of God, seen in the mercy seat, man was able to commune with God.

Such a brief summary of the tabernacle certainly does not do the topic justice, but perhaps it has briefed us enough so that we can make several observations relative to praise and worship:

When we worship God, we worship Him in our spirits.

In one respect, the tabernacle is a type of the Christian. Indeed, Paul said, "Do you not know that you are a temple of God, and that the Spirit of God dwells in you?" (1 Cor. 3:16). Just as the tabernacle had three distinct parts, the Christian has a body, soul, and spirit. The body corresponds to the Outer Court; it is visible to all and responds to natural light and the physical environment. Our soul is analogous to the Holy Place. Within our mind, will and emotions, we fellowship with believers and receive mental nourishment (shewbread); we walk based on artificial light (lampstand); and we praise and pray (altar of incense). Our spirit links us to the divine: when Christ comes to dwell in our lives, He abides in our spirit. "God is spirit; and those who worship Him must worship in spirit . . ." (John 4:24).

The priest administered many religious duties in the Outer Court and Holy Place, but it was in the Holy of Holies that he met God. Likewise, we can become engaged in many religious activities which are good and proper and even necessary, but if we stop short of the Holy of Holies, we will miss communion with God. As Christians, we must become sensitive to the difference between activity of the soul and consciousness of the spirit. This is part of the work of the Word of God in our lives (Heb. 4:12). We must learn to isolate the presence and innate functions of the spirit, and then pursue them to find the presence of the living God.

We have the joyous privilege of coming boldly before the throne of grace (Heb. 4:16).

To the children of Israel, the presence of God was to be enjoyed once a year, by only one person, the high priest. Furthermore, the high priest entered His presence with such fear and trepidation that he wore bells on the bottom of his robe and a rope around his ankle, for fear that if he were found unworthy, the Lord would kill him and he would have to be dragged away under the veil.

Because of Christ's work on the cross, the veil of the Temple was rent in two from top to bottom. Now, through the shed blood of Christ we have direct and unrestrained access to the presence and worship of God.

The tabernacle procedure is a step-by-step process for entering Christian fullness and a holy life of praise and worship.

We enter the life of Christ through the straight and narrow gate. Within the courtyard we come under the influence of biblical teaching and companionship. We must daily go to the altar of sacrifice and receive the cleansing blood of Christ for our sins. Christ, by His death, once for all satisfied the need for blood sacrifice: "He made Him who knew no sin to be sin on our behalf, that we might become the righteousness of God in Him" (2 Cor. 5:21). At the altar, we also consecrate ourselves to Him, acknowledging His claim on our lives: "to present your bodies a living and holy sacrifice, acceptable to God" (Rom. 12:1).

The laver is where we go for sanctification, putting to death the flesh, and receiving the Spirit. "Those who are in the flesh cannot please God . . . for if you are living according to the flesh, you must die; but if by the Spirit you are putting to death the deeds of the body, you will live" (Rom. 8:8, 13).

Next we come to the table of shewbread, where we receive the daily bread so necessary for spiritual nourishment and growth. This bread, made from "fine flour," is none other than Jesus who said, "I am the living bread . . . if anyone eats of this bread, he shall live forever" (John 6:51). It is also the place of fellowship with the saints, for our fellowship is "with the Father, and with His Son Jesus Christ" (1 John 1:3).

The lampstand is our place of illumination. Jesus said, "I am the light of the world: he that followeth me shall not walk in darkness" (John 8:12 KJV). God's Holy Word is a lamp to our feet, and a light to our path (Ps. 119:105). To be effective in our Christian walk, we must walk in the light. A daily trip to God's Word and dependence on the revelation of Jesus will give us this needed guidance.

At the altar of incense we pray and praise. Along with the Psalmist we say, "May my prayer be counted as incense before Thee; The lifting up of my hands as the evening offering" (Ps. 141:2). Our praise of God should be like a soothing aroma, pleasing to Him and blessing those who are around us.

The six activities stated above were part of the daily routine of the ministering priests. How effective our lives would be if we made them an integral part of our daily lives and practices. Though most of the priests had to stop in the Holy Place, we can continue on to the mercy seat, as did the high priest, where real communion with God is consummated. Many Christians, for various reasons, are not determined enough to enter the Holy of Holies. They are satisifed to participate in the six activities leading up to worship: but they are hesitant to really enter in. I have noticed this quite often in a worship service. During the praise part of the service many folks will avidly participate, but when the "holy hush" comes and the Spirit attempts to perform an intimate work, some refuse to proceed. Worship is a time to receive life and revelation from God. Our spirits need worship in order to survive and thrive.

What an extreme privilege we have in our ability to worship in such freedom. Of the entire nation of Israel, only one man, the high priest, was able to come before the throne of God, and then only once a year, and with fear and trembling. Even with such free access to the presence of God, we should enter with the same sense of awe as did the high priest. God is the same today as He was then. What a privilege to worship Him!

29
Praise the Name of the Lord

> As is Thy name, O God, so is Thy praise to the ends of the earth (Ps. 48:10).

There is a significant relationship between the name of God and the praise of God. The alliance between the two is seen throughout the Bible. In this verse, the psalmist developed a strong correlation between the proclamation of God's name throughout the earth and the praise of the Lord to the ends of the earth.

Before several observations are made on this particular verse, it should be noted that in Hebrew the word "name" does not simply mean the name by which a person is called (Paul, John); it means the nature, the character, or the personality of the person. We can observe several Scriptures to better understand how the biblical writers used this term.

"Some boast in chariots, and some in horses; but we will boast in the name of the Lord, our God" (Ps. 20:7). In a time of trouble, the psalmist says, some people put their trust in the power of human resources, but we will put our trust in the character, nature, divine attributes, and power of God, as He has revealed himself to us. It is obvious he is not implying that our trust is in the letters of the name *Jehovah*.

"The Lord gave and the Lord has taken away. Blessed be the name of the Lord" (Job 1:21). Job praised the omnipotence of God and His privilege to give and to take away as He desires. He remembered what God is like, and that recollection brought him confidence and assurance.

"O Lord, our Lord, how majestic is Thy name in all the earth" (Ps. 8:1). Here the psalmist was testifying to the greatness of the Lord's name and how that greatness extends to all the earth. He was boasting of the mighty character and nature of God.

Whenever we see the word "name" used in the Old Testament, we need to expand our usage of the term to include all that God is and all He will be for us in any given circumstance.

With this understanding in mind, several observations can be made regarding Psalm 48:10:

Wherever the name of God is pronounced, praise will also be manifest.

It is impossible for the power of God to be displayed without praise erupting soon after. The very nature of God demands that we bow before Him in reverential awe. When the mouth of Zacharias was opened, upon the miraculous birth of his son, he immediately began to speak in praise of God (Luke 1:64). Even the heathen King Nebuchadnezzar, upon seeing the protective hand of God on His loved ones, blessed the Lord and proclaimed, "His kingdom is an everlasting kingdom" (Dan. 4:3). There is no more proper, suitable or appropriate activity in the presence of God than praise. It is perhaps the one action that we can feel most comfortable performing in His presence. Our first and finest response to the ways of God in our midst is praise. In heaven, where the name of God is highly exalted, His praise never ceases (Rev. 4:8).

The whole earth will hear the name of God, and consequently the whole earth will praise Him.

It is just a matter of time until the prophecy of Malachi is fulfilled: "For from the rising of the sun, even to its setting, My name will be great among the nations, and in every place incense is going to be offered to My Name . . . for My Name will be great among the nations" (Mal. 1:11). In that day, "at the name of Jesus, every knee will bow, of those who are in heaven, and on earth, and under the earth" (see Phil. 2:10). In that day, the whole earth will be filled with the praise of God. The statement made by the chief musician in Psalm 145:21 will come to fruition: "And all flesh will bless His holy name forever and ever."

The time when all mankind will praise Him is yet to come, but even now the created universe acknowledges the reigning Lord. I believe that when the psalmist invoked the whole of creation to praise to the Lord (Ps. 150), he was not just being poetic, but touching reality and demanding something that can be delivered. The stars of heaven, the waters, the snow, the fruit trees, the cattle, all offer, in their own way, praise to the Lord.

The name of God is the basis of our praise.

There are numerous names given to the Trinity throughout the Bible. These names, divinely conceived, reveal different aspects of the character, nature, and actions of God the Father, the Son, and the Holy Spirit. These names are the foundation of our praise and worship. They are also the source upon which we draw when we have a special need in our lives.

When you are sick and are in need of the healing touch of God, pray to *Jehovah-rophe,* the God who heals. When you are distraught, pray for the Comforter to meet your needs. Praising Emmanuel (which means "God is with us") will reassure your heart of God's presence and His commitment to never leave or forsake us.

Many parents do not even bother to discover the meaning of the names they give to their children, much less select a name for their child because of a significant meaning it may possess. This was not the case in biblical times. Names were very important.

- Hagar, Sarai's maid, named her firstborn "Ishmael," meaning "God hears," because the Lord gave heed to her affliction.
- Abraham's firstborn by Sarah was named "Isaac," meaning "he laughs," because Abraham laughed at God's message that he would father a son in his old age.
- Leah named her firstborn "Reuben," meaning "see, a son," because she hoped to gain Jacob's favor by giving him a son.
- God changed Abram's name meaning "exalted father" to "Abraham," which means "father of a multitude," because of God's promise that he would be the father of many nations.
- Jesus changed Simon's name to "Peter," meaning "a stone," because of his eventual strong faith in Christ.

It is no wonder that God has given Jesus many titles to describe the many facets of His character and ministry. He has many appellations because His abilities are without measure.

I have a personal conviction regarding the name of our Lord. When the angel appeared to Mary and Joseph, he said, "You shall bear a Son, and you shall call His name Jesus" (Matt. 1:21 and Luke 1:31). The name God chose for His incarnate Son was "Jesus." *That* is the name of the Lord! He may have many titles, depending upon the particular way in which He is manifested (e.g., Teacher, Physician, Wonderful Counsellor, Shepherd), but He has only one name, and that is the name Jesus! In like manner, I may be called father, husband, friend, teacher, minister, or other titles depending upon the circumstances, but my name is Don.

We must always feel free to call upon any of the titles by which Jesus is recognized. This can be of particular value when a specific need is present. For instance, when you are ill, call upon Jesus the Physician. Yet we must always bear in mind that His name is Jesus. It is that name which God has highly exalted and it is at the name of Jesus that every knee will bow! That name should flow freely from our lips; we should call upon that name for all our needs. Indeed, it is by the name of Jesus that we:

> are saved (Acts 4:12; Rom. 10:13)
> are baptized (Acts 19:5)
> are healed (James 5:14; Acts 3:6)
> perform miracles (Mark 9:39)
> gather together (Matt. 18:20)
> pray (John 14:13, 14)

receive the Holy Spirit (John 14:16)
   are kept (John 17:11)
   are called (James 2:7)
   perform all Christian service (Col. 3:17)
   cast out demons (Mark 16:17)

His name is worthy of our praise!

Listed below are just a few of the many names of God recorded in Scripture. Pray using these names, claim the provision provided by the names, and let them be the basis upon which you praise Him:

Father

Elohim-The one to whom all power belongs (Gen. 1:1).
El Roi-The God who continually sees (Gen. 16:13).
El Olam-The everlasting God (Isa. 40:28).
Adonai-A helper in time of need (Gen. 15:2).
Jehovah sabaoth-The Lord of hosts (1 Sam. 1:3).
Jehovah jireh-The Lord will provide (Gen. 22:14).
Jehovah rophe-The Lord that heals (Exod. 15:26).
Jehovah nissi-The Lord is my banner (Exod. 17:15).
Jehovah rohi-The Lord is my shepherd (Ps. 23:1).
Jehovah shalom-The Lord is my peace (Judg. 6:24).
Jehovah Tsidkenu-The Lord is my righteousness (Jer. 23:6).
Jehovah Shammeh-The Lord is there (Ezek. 48:35).

Son Messiah, Rose of Sharon, Wonderful Counselor, Prince of Peace, Bright and Morning Star, Teacher, Lamb of God, Master, Christ, Lion of the Tribe of Judah.

Holy Spirit Comforter, Teacher, Truth, Giver of Gifts, The Promise, The One Who Bears Witness.

30
Vain Worship

True worship is a wonderful experience—we focus on the person of God and enter the flow of His life. Having worshiped, we are never the same. Whenever we come into the presence of the living God and our spirits are touched by the divine fire, we will inevitably be changed. Our perspective on life will be different, our priorities will re-align, and our actions, attitudes and speech will be altered to come into consonance with His will.

To the same degree in which true worship is advantageous to our lives, vain worship is detrimental and futile. Throughout history, untold scores of people have invested years of their lives going through a form of worship but never touching the living God. Some are deceived as to the necessary means of approaching God; some have sincere aspirations but are sincerely wrong. Such worship is futile because it fails to relate us to God, and it is detrimental because we can waste much time thinking that we are communicating with Him, when actually all we are participating in is fruitless forms of worship.

There are three main areas of vain worship, three basic mistakes we can make in our attempt to reach the Almighty: to worship anything but the living God; for an unregenerated person to attempt to commune with God; and for the believer to attempt to worship with sin in his heart.

Our worship must be directed only toward the living God:

> You shall have no other gods before Me. You shall not make for yourself an idol, or any likeness of what is in heaven above or on the earth beneath or in the water under the earth. You shall not worship them or serve them; for I, the Lord your God, am a jealous God, visiting the iniquity of the fathers on the children, on the third and the fourth generations of those who hate Me (Exod. 20:3-5).

The first command the Lord gave the children of Israel upon their exodus from Egypt concerned worship. He warned them that they would be tempted to give homage to other gods, particularly ones they could see and touch (Deut. 4:15-20; Exod. 34:14). God is a jealous God, especially toward His own people, and it is a serious offense to worship someone or something other than Him. This is evident in 1 Kings 18, the story of Elijah's contest with the prophets of Baal and Asherah. The Asherah was a wooden symbol of a female deity. Baal was the god of fertility with the bull as its symbol. These priests worshiped them, perhaps untold hours a day, but their worship was in vain. Even when they cut their own bodies and spilled their blood, their worship was useless. All their activity, the jumping about the altar, their raving and prophecy, was nonsense because they were attempting to worship an inanimate object. Often we are no less guilty in our devotion to things that we place above our devotion to God. A car, a house, a child or a spouse, all are subject to becoming idols in our lives. The greatest area of danger lies in our love of self. The most subtle area of idolatry lies in a love of church activity or programs, or perhaps the church building itself. These are equally detestable in the eyes of the Lord.

For our worship to be effective, it must be centered on the living Lord. In our worship services, a personality, a building-fund drive, a new program, or any other thing must not be elevated above the person of Christ. If one is, our worship will be in vain.

When the apostle John was receiving his revelation from God, he no doubt was in a state of spiritual ecstasy. John, the apostle for whom Jesus had a special love (John 13:23, 19:26), was near the end of a long and fruitful life spent in service for the Lord. He was probably as spiritually mature as a human can become. Yet, in the midst of the revelation he was guilty of vain worship:

> And I, John, am the one who heard and saw these things. And when I heard and saw, I fell down to worship at the feet of the angel who showed me these things. And he said to me, "Do not do that; I am a fellow servant of yours and of your brethren the prophets and of those who heed the words of this book; worship God" (Rev. 22:8, 9).

Peter fell into this error on the Mount of Transfiguration. Jesus was transformed before his very eyes. The appearance of Christ's face became different, and His garments became exceedingly white. At that moment Elijah and Moses appeared with the Lord and they began discussing the events which were to soon transpire in Jerusalem. When Peter saw and heard this transcendent incident he opened his mouth (a bad habit he seemed to possess) and said, "Rabbi, it is good for us to be here; let us make three tabernacles, one for You, and one for Moses, and one for Elijah" (Mark 9:5). The problem with Peter's unpremeditated comment lies in the fact that tabernacles are places of worship. Peter's suggestion that three tabernacles be built implied that he viewed the three men as being equal; he wanted to worship all three. God the Father quickly dealt with the very suggestion of false worship. A cloud immediately formed, Moses and Elijah were removed from view, and God audibly declared the uniqueness of His Son, "This is My beloved Son, listen to Him!"

We are surely just as susceptible to such an error. If we are not cautious, we can find ourselves paying homage to a man who indeed may be our spiritual elder. We can respect such persons, but must not worship them. There is also a message here for persons in positions of spiritual leadership. The angel did not allow, for one moment, John's vain worship. Rather, he immediately pointed John's worship toward God. There are some who enjoy the adoration given by those around them, but it is sin for both parties, and God will not tolerate such activity.

Worship can only be entered into by those who have been regenerated, that is, those who have put their trust in Jesus and have received the cleansing of His blood. This simply means that a non-Christian cannot worship. Furthermore, a Christian who has known sin in his life cannot enter into communion with God.

Vain Worship

In Exodus, chapter 30, the contents of the holy anointing oil are given in minute detail. The oil is symbolic of the anointing of theHoly Spirit for the service of worship. Three sacred restrictions are given as to its use on humans:

> And thou shalt anoint Aaron and his sons, and consecrate them, that they may minister unto me in the priest's office. And thou shalt speak unto the children of Israel, saying, "This shall be a holy anointing oil unto me throughout your generations. Upon man's flesh shall it not be poured, neither shall ye make any other like it, after the composition of it: it is holy, and it shall be holy unto you. Whosoever compoundeth any like it, or whosoever putteth any of it upon a stronger, shall even be cut off from his people (Exod. 30:30-33 KJV).

"Upon man's flesh it shall not be poured." This is the error of attempting to exalt the carnal man, lifting up natural talents or abilities which a man may possess. Some churches will highly advertise the coming of a movie star or athlete even though the individual may be a new Christian or not be totally committed to the life style of Jesus. In some cases, they are notoriously worldly people. This is exalting man's flesh; this is pouring holy oil on the flesh. I have become more and more convinced through the years that the key to spiritual ministry is a holy life style. God cannot and will not bless man's flesh. I have often noticed the difference between singing a song in the spirit and in the flesh. Two different individuals, regardless of musical ability, sing the same song, but one ministered life and the other entertained. One nourished our spirits, the other excited our souls. In choosing individuals to minister in our services, the question should not be "Are they well-known?" or "Are they talented?", but rather, "Are they right with God and do they have a fresh touch from the throne?"

"Whosoever putteth any of it upon a stranger." This is the sin of putting into a position of prominence those who have not been regenerated. In our churches, if a man is wealthy, or influential, or well-respected in the community, we may call upon him to direct a campaign, or to pray or speak at a dedication service but not question his walk with the Lord. We may seek a musician because of his musical ability, not because he confesses Christ as Savior. The unsaved have no business attempting to do the work of ministry. It is not only fruitless, but an abomination to the Lord (v. 33).

"Whosoever compoundeth any like it." If the spirit of God does not rest upon our assembling together, or His blessing is not evident on one of our programs or projects, we will often attempt to artificially imitate the anointing of God. We will devise all sorts of clever psychology, hire a public relations firm, or juggle statistics in order to imitate the anointing of God. The Lord makes it very clear that there is but one Holy Spirit and that He controls the anointing and the outpouring. It is interesting to note that God made the formula of the anointing oil general knowledge. It was not hard to copy the ingredients and their measurements, but having the right formula would not ensure the presence of God's spirit, it would be just another perfume oil. How often we falsely rely on formulas for spiritual success when only the presence of God brings spiritual prosperity.

The believer cannot worship with sin in his heart. The interdependence of righteousness and praise was covered in chapter four. I mention this important correlation simply

Vain Worship

to say that we Christians worship in vain if we are not clean vessels before the Lord. If we attempt to approach the presence of God with sin in our lives, His presence will not be found among us. This too is vain worship. If we are not careful, we may sin in a very subtle way, during the very act of worship. In Matthew 6, the Lord gives three acts of worship which must be done in private or else they will be done in vain: giving, praying and fasting.

> But when you give alms, do not let your left hand know what your right hand is doing that your alms may be in secret; and your Father who sees in secret will repay you . . . And when you pray, go into your inner room, and when you have shut your door, pray to your Father who is in secret, and your Father who sees in secret will repay you . . . When you fast, anoint your head, and wash your face so that you may not be seen fasting by men, but by your Father who is in secret; and your Father who sees in secret will repay you (Matt. 6:3, 6, 17).

Worship is important—without it our spiritual lives dry up and become encrusted with knowledge that lacks power. However, we must not only worship God, but we must worship Him according to His design, prompted and guided by His Spirit. To do otherwise is an exercise in futility.

31
Evangelism and Praise

Evangelism is a high priority of the New Testament church. It is the one activity of the church that will not exist in heaven; all the evangelism to be done must be rendered during this life. An evidence of one who is wholly given to the Lord is a burden for the lost and a life style directed to bringing the lost to Christ. We often think that the ministry of evangelism and the ministry of praise and worship are mutually exclusive, one focusing on the lost man and the other on the Christian. But in truth, they are complementary and one can be used to magnify the effectiveness of the other.

Christ is magnificent! His deeds, His ways, His mannerisms, the words He speaks, the way He looks, His response to any given situation; He is excellent and attractive in every way! Therefore, in New Testament evangelism, we do not need to sell people on Jesus, we need to show people Jesus. He does not need a defense lawyer, He needs a dynamic witness who will uphold His glorious personage. Christ himself is the focal point of salvation. In Him we see our need for salvation (due to His holiness), and in Him we see the provision for salvation (His sacrifice at Calvary). Though the fear of hell, or a tragic event, may lead us to Christ, it is ultimately the love of Christ and the efficacy of His shed blood to which we are drawn.

This is why praise is such a powerful tool for evangelism. In praise, we are lifting up Jesus. We are magnifying His character and His ability to meet our needs, and we are testifying of His past faithfulness. Psalm 136 is a praise history of the life of the children of Israel; every other phrase is a refrain of praise, "For His lovingkindness is everlasting." When hearing this song the heathen have to stand in awe of a God so great.

I have been in praise services in which Jesus was so exalted and made so real that the lost could do nothing else but come to Him. They were attracted to a living Christ because they saw the sincere praise of His followers. They could not help but see the admiration and devotion with which His children approached Him. Simply stated, as Christ was lifted up in their midst, they could see no one but Him. The lost person needs to see Jesus as Isaiah did, "high and lifted up." The stone-hearted Saul of Tarsus was converted when he saw and heard the magnificent Christ. We need not beg or plead with the unconverted; we simply need to point them to Jesus. Christ inhabits our praise, and the lost are convicted of their need for Christ when we praise Him. I have been involved in personal witnessing experiences in which the prospect, for some reason, just could not make a decision for Christ. Right in the middle of the sharing time I would lead in a time of praise and usually sufficient freedom would be granted for the person to respond to Christ.

Evangelism and Praise

There are many ways to determine if a Christian or a church is cold, hot, or lukewarm (Rev. 3:15-16). A prime indicator is the spirit of the worship service. A church living in the fullness of the Holy Spirit will naturally want to enter praise and do so in a grand manner. "Great is the Lord, and greatly to be praised" (Ps. 48:1). But, to the contrary, it is very difficult to get a backslider to verbally express himself to God, particularly in the midst of the congregation. God would have us confess Him freely. We often think that we should not be too verbal in our use of the Lord's name or in praise, so as not to offend the lost one or run him off. Quite the opposite is true. That lost person needs to see and hear an unashamed and zealous confession of our love for the Lord. It will do nothing but convince him of the reality of the God we serve.

A brief perusal of the early church will reveal many instances in which praise and evangelism were nearly synonymous.

In Acts 2, the disciples of Christ were obediently waiting for the promise of the Spirit. When He came, the early church was born in a flurry of power and excitement and the disciples began to speak the "mighty deeds of God." When they became full of the Spirit of God, they began praising Him! They were unashamed and unintimidated in this new experience. As a result of this outpouring, the praise service, and Peter's sermon, three thousand souls were saved and baptized in one day. This is a good order of worship: outpouring of God's Spirit, praise, anointed preaching.

In Acts 13, God's appointment of the first missionaries and their ordination came in the midst of a praise gathering. The church at Antioch was "ministering to the Lord and fasting" (v. 2) when the Holy Spirit instructed that Barnabas and Saul be set aside to do the work of missionary evangelists.

Though praise may not always precede salvation, it inevitably follows it. When the word of salvation was preached to the Gentiles, many believed, and they began "rejoicing and glorifying the Word of the Lord" (v. 48).

The heart that worships God is a tender heart and one that is open to the revelation of God. This is shown in Acts 16 in the life of a woman named Lydia, for she was a "worshiper of God." As she listened to Paul preach the good news of salvation through Jesus, the Lord "opened her heart to respond to the things spoken by Paul (v. 14). Lydia was saved, and her household. A similar story is seen in Luke 7 where the immoral woman came and worshiped at the feet of Jesus. She had a tender heart. She left the house saved; the Lord's host, Simon the Pharisee, who did not even offer the Lord a traditional foot-bathing, remained cold in his heart, and lost!

The salvation of the Philippian jailer and his household was preceded by a praise service led by Paul and Silas as they were "praying and singing hymns of praise to God" while in jail (Acts 16:25). Though the jailer did not hear the singing, he became consumed by the power of God which inhabited that praise.

Not only is praise a tremendous tool of evangelism, but the fruits of evangelism provide the impetus for a great praise service. Luke 15:10 says that there is joy in the presence of the angels of God over one sinner who repents. The corridors of heaven are filled with angelic praise when salvation transpires in the heart of a mortal. This is somewhat strange considering that the holy angels cannot

Evangelism and Praise

fully understand or appreciate the depths of salvation, because they have not been washed in the blood of Jesus. I believe they rejoice because they see the great joy the Father has when one is born again. They see Jesus rejoice because His shed blood has provided atonement for yet another, and the Holy Spirit's work of convicting men of sin is brought to happy fruition once again. Evangelistic churches usually have a high level of praise, because there is a constant stream of new life.

I honestly do not believe we possess the necessary power to evangelize until we have worshiped God. Evangelism should spring forth from an overflow in our lives. This filling to capacity comes from worship. Without a fresh touch from the Lord, evangelism is an obligation rather than an opportunity; we begin to function out of guilt instead of joy.

There seems to be a pattern established in the Bible in regard to worship and evangelism; the pattern is worship first and then go. The famous commission found in Matthew 28:19-20, "Go ye therefore . . ." is preceeded by the experience of Matthew 28:17, "And when they saw Him, they worshiped Him." The fact that the disciples saw Jesus and worshiped Him gave them the needed impetus to go into the world. Note the testimony of the prophet, Jonah. Jonah received a commission from the Lord, "Arise, go to Ninevah . . ." but failed miserably, "But Jonah rose up to flee to Tarshish." However, prior to the next call of God, Jonah had a worship experience. Right in the stomach of that large fish, Jonah met God and proclaimed, "But I will sacrifice to Thee with the voice of thanksgiving. That which I have vowed I will pay. Salvation is from the Lord" (Jonah 2:9). Chapter 3 records the post-worship encounter. "Now the word of the Lord came to Jonah the second time saying,

'Arise, go to Ninevah' . . . so Jonah arose and went to Ninevah . . . then the people of Ninevah believed in God" (vv. 1-5). What a striking illustration of what an encounter with God will do for our evangelistic zeal!

Salvation and praise are always seen together, because they both originate and culminate in the love of God for a lost world. Have you bragged of Jesus today to a lost friend? Has that lost neighbor seen your heart full of praise though your circumstances may be trying? Have you praised Him today for saving your soul? We can testify, along with the song-writer:

> I will praise Him, I will praise Him.
> Praise the Lamb for sinners slain.
> Give Him glory all ye people,
> For His blood has washed away my stain.
> —Harris

32
Restful Worship

Have you ever noticed in a praise service, while many may be doing basically the same thing, singing the same songs, listening to the same testimonies, inevitably some go away blessed and others just go away? Some are just going through the motions while others are having an encounter with God. Obviously, there are many reasons why such a problem occurs. An individual may be apathetic toward the Lord; there may be unconfessed sin prohibiting communion; fear or intimidation may be present.

Another common hindrance, one which is very subtle in its error, is making praise and worship an act of work rather than an act of faith. Scripture instructs us, "For by grace you have been saved through faith; and that not of yourselves, it is the gift of God; not as a result of works, that no one should boast" (Eph. 2:8, 9); and, "As ye have therefore received Christ Jesus the Lord, so walk ye in Him" (Col. 2:6 KJV). We were not saved by any work of our own; likewise, we cannot accomplish anything in our Christian life except by faith. Even our praise life must be a faith life or else it will be in vain. The praise of many saints is fruitless because they have a wrong mindset, attempting to please or appease God through works, in this case, the very act of praise, when in reality it is the presence of faith that pleases God (Heb. 11:6).

In 2 Corinthians 11:3, Paul expressed a deep concern for the church at Corinth: "But I am afraid, lest as the serpent deceived Eve by his craftiness, your minds should be led astray from the simplicity and purity of devotion to Christ." Paul was afraid that these immature saints were being deceived and led astray by the same lie and deception by which Eve was victimized. The devil was up to his age-old trick. What lie of Satan caused Eve to stumble? Genesis 3:4, 5 tells us the answer: "And the serpent said to the woman, 'You surely shall not die! For God knows that in the day you eat from it your eyes will be opened, and you will be like God, knowing good and evil.' "

Satan told Eve that she had to *do something* in order to be like God, when in fact, she already was like God! God had fashioned her in His image (Gen. 1:26), and they had intimate communion (Gen. 1:26-29). Herein we have the foundational lie upon which many false religions are based. It is a "works" ethic. It is the idea that we have to do something in order to be accepted by God, we have to strive to be like Him, when in reality we are like Him, through the work of Christ. This was the sin of Cain; he thought an offering from the fruit of his own labor would satisfy God. God said that only the gift of Abel, which represented the work of Christ, would be acceptable.

One of the most liberating discoveries we can make in the Christian life is to realize who we are. God says that we are "holy and blameless and beyond reproach" (Col. 1:22); we are "chosen of God, holy and beloved" (Col. 3:12);

we are "qualified . . . to share in the inheritance" (Col. 1:12); we are "seated" with Christ "in the heavenly places" (Eph. 2:6); and that we have entered into rest and have ceased from our labors (Heb. 4:9, 10).

In Romans 8, Paul asked, "Who will bring a charge against God's elect?" (v. 33). Who has the right to condemn me? Who can question my worth? Jeuss Christ is the only one who has this right (v. 34). Where then is Christ? He is seated at the right hand of God, making intercession for us (v. 34). The only one who can judge us is praying for us! Beloved, our position in Christ is very sure!

In our church, we sing a chorus entitled "And Because We Are Sons." The lyrics are taken directly from Galatians 4:6, "And because we are sons, God has sent forth the Spirit of His Son into our hearts, crying, 'Abba Father!' " Abba is an Aramaic word (the language spoken by Jews in Palestine in the first century) which expresses an affectionate fondness, an intimate filial relationship to God. It can be translated "Daddy" or "Papa." Jesus used the expression when He was in the Garden of Gethsemane (Mark 14:36). It is a beautiful verse which speaks of our intimate relationship to God. When we approach Him in prayer, because of the presence of the indwelling Spirit, we can call Him "Daddy, God." It almost sounds disrespectful, but it is certainly our right and privilege.

We must never approach praise with the attitude that it will improve our standing with God or that it will make us more acceptable to Him. We are already accepted and we stand as sons before a loving Father. We do not praise Him out of obligation or with the thought that our worth will be increased. Instead, we praise Him on the basis of who he is and who we have become. My two daughters do not have to work for my love and acceptance; it is already theirs. I do desire, however, their love and fellowship.

For some, praise has become just another area of performance, another vain attempt to become what God has already declared we are. In truth, we should approach praise in confidence, realizing who we are in Christ. We should feel comfortable, welcome, and at rest in our praise experience. We are not on a performance basis; we are beloved and accepted. Several months ago I ran across this simple definition of worship. It seemed too simple at first glance, but the more I think about it, the more it seems to capture the real essence of our coming to Him:

> **Worship** is not a vain compliment, but the uninhibited hug of a child for his father.

33
The Highest Praise

The highest praise . . . is to give my life to you.
—Waters/Cox

There are many expressions of praise. Often we sing as an act of praise; sometimes we pray silently. Some people are led to clap, or shout, or lift holy hands to the Lord as an expression of praise. As a matter of fact, there is no such thing as a "rubber stamp" approach to praise and worship. The Bible never says you must do this or that in order to praise God. Instead, it gives many variables, many elements by which we can express ourselves. This provides freshness in worship and places a high premium on creativity. This also underscores the danger of judging other people regarding their mode of worship. One cannot think that his praise is more intense than another because he lifts his hands while the other does not. Sincere praise can only be measured in the heavens.

An important expression of praise is obedience. When we act in obedience to the Lord's plan for our lives, we are a living testimony of praise. In essence, we praise Him by being who He wants us to be and doing what He wants us to do. When we are what He created us to be, our lives are a declaration of His glory. This explains the essence of Psalm 148 in which many inanimate objects are commanded to praise the Lord: "Praise the Lord! . . . Praise Him, sun and moon . . . fire and hail, snow and clouds . . ."

How can fire, or the sun and moon, praise the Lord? They praise Him by doing what they were created to do. When the sun obediently functions in its assigned capacity in the universe, it honors the God who made it. The beauty and function of fire, hail, and snow fulfill His Word, and in so doing give glory to the Creator. In like manner, our lives praise God through our obedience. I believe the children of Israel were in a state of praise as they marched seven times around Jericho. The entire ordeal had a tenor of celebration. Many no doubt were questioning, "Why march around the walls seven times?" Though not understanding why, they were obedient, and their obedience pleased God and brought about a great victory. In small issues as well as large issues, whether the obedience is seen by men or is noticed only by God, obedience is indicative of our love for Him and is a means of expressing our adoration.

Though obedience is a high level of praise, there is yet a greater expression. One song says it this way:

> Lofty words, pious repetitions,
> Phrases great and grand are not
>   what He demands . . .
> . . . I will praise Him, knowing
> that my praise will cost me
> everything.

The Highest Praise

The most important, encompassing and effective way to praise and worship God is to give our lives to Him; a total, unabandoned release of all we are to Him. If we sincerely acknowledge Him as the supreme potentate of the universe, a lesser expression of praise will not be acceptable. Drawing again from the song:

> Were the whole realm of nature mine,
> That were a present far too small,
> Love so amazing so divine,
> Demands my soul, my life, my all!

Some saints will come into the sanctuary and give many external signs of worship, but if their life is not committed totally to Him there is a disavowing discrepancy between actions and heart commitment. What benefits is there in our worship service if we loudly sing songs of praise but know in our hearts that when the invitation is given we may not be willing to say yes to everything God may call us to do? In Matthew two, the Magi stated that they had traveled from the East looking for the King of the Jews that they might worship Him. In the same chapter, Herod also verbally indicated a desire to worship the Christ child—but what a contrast between the hearts of these men! Both confessed worship, but one with hate and murder in his heart, the others with sincere worship and adoration.

Abraham is a prime example of a man whose worship was supported by a life totally given to God. In the stirring account of the proposed sacrifice of his son Isaac (Gen. 22), Abraham considered the whole incident an act of worship: "Stay here with the donkey, and I and the lad will go yonder; and we will worship and return to you" (v. 5). Abraham was prepared for true worship because he was prepared to offer to the Lord anything He demanded. To sacrifice the life of his son was no doubt more of an offering than to give his own life. When Abraham "stretched out his hand, and took the knife to slay his son," he died to all his status, his ambition, family, everything. God did not require from Abraham the life of his son, but if God had, He would have received it. I believe Abraham was at total peace during the entire ordeal. He did not dread to give what God had required, but was totally confident in the wisdom and counsel of God. So confident was he in the promise of God that he said to his servant "wait here and *we* will worship *and return."* There is a great lesson to learn by this example. Those who worship the Lord and know Him have no reservation about committing their lives to Him. They have seen Him and are confident in His counsel. However, many have spent so little time in His presence and are so unfamiliar with the Lord's ways that they are hesitant to give Him control of their lives. Worship fosters commitment.

I recently finished reading the biography of Rees Howell written by Norman Grubb. Rees Howell was a man totally committed to God. This uneducated Welsh coal miner prompted the great Welsh Revival and perhaps changed the history of the world through his prayers and the prayers of his students. His life was a living sacrifice of praise. His total obedience to Christ was a dynamic, constant and enduring act of worship. Though Mr. Howell has long been deceased, his earthly life continues to honor Christ because of its inspiration to others. This man worshiped God through total commitment.

Romans twelve describes the act of worship with which God is well-pleased: "I urge you therefore, brethren, by the mercies of God, to present your bodies a living and holy sacrifice, acceptable to God, which is your spiritual service of worship" (v. 1).

When Paul penned these words to the believers at Rome, they no doubt had a startling effect. They were acquainted only with the animal sacrifices required under Jewish law. Here Paul urged the saints to present *themselves* as sacrifices—their own bodies. I am sure the addition of the two qualifying adjectives "living and holy" were received with a sigh of relief.

The term "living sacrifice" seems to be a paradox. In temple worship the one presenting the offering would place his hands on the head of the animal, thereby transferring to God all his right, title, and investment in the sacrifice, and then present the animal to the priest to be slain. There were no living sacrifices!

The essence of Paul's message is self-denial to the point of dying to self. He said the same thing in a different way in Galatians 2:20, "I have been crucified with Christ; and it is no longer I who live," and in 1 Corinthians 15:31, "I die daily." The sacrifice of atonement was made once for all by the death of Christ, but the sacrifice of acknowledgment is necessary daily. We present our bodies as a living sacrifice when we relinquish our desires in order to accept His likings, when we abrogate our will for His, and when we abandon all rights to everything we own and influence. In short, when we give Him our all.

God calls this worship! He calls it spiritual worship, perhaps the zenith of worship. It is one thing to give an animal in worship; it is yet another to give yourself. Do you want to worship God right now? Crawl upon the altar and die. And in so dying, live for the glory and praise of Jesus.

34
Leading People in Worship

We are all believer-priests, and as such do not need another human being to be our intermediary to bring us to God. We are all welcome to come and partake freely of the river of life; we are even told to come boldly before the throne of God. It seems, however, that when we meet together, God has designed that someone lead in the time of praise and worship. When our gathering is small and intimate and everyone present knows how to follow the leading of the Spirit, a leader is not as necessary, but in most cases God chooses to work through an individual in leadership.

It is an awesome task to lead people in worship. It demands such a sensitivity to the Spirit. A great sense of responsibility accompanies the authority and privilege. In chapter four we discussed the necessity of righteousness in praise. This applies strongly to those leading others in praise. Additionally, there must be clear communication between the Holy Spirit, who is the master of ceremonies in all worship services, and the leader. Though planning may be led by the Spirit, the service must also be marked by spontaneity.

All this is to say that the worship leader must take his ministry very seriously and must be spiritually prepared for the task. Spurgeon once said, "The man who guides others into the presence of the King must have journied far into the King's country and oft looked upon His face." The only thing that really qualifies a man to lead in corporate worship is the experience of having met God in private worship. It is not a man's talents that make him able to lead in worship; ability to sing, teach, or speak are inadequate in themselves to prepare one for the task of worship. Sometimes an excessive amount of talent can even be a negative factor because of the tendency to rely on man's flesh. A worship leader must have a face-to-face confrontation with God in his private devotions and then be able to carry that experience with him into the place of corporate worship. There is always a shallow feeling of inadequacy when this does not happen. People will follow a leader much quicker and with more confidence if they are certain that the leader has already been where he wants to lead them.

All of God's great leaders had first-hand experience with the Lord. For Joshua, it came when he met the "captain of the host of the Lord" (Josh. 5:13-15); Jacob wrestled with an angel and confessed that he had seen God face-to-face (Gen. 32:24-30); Moses encountered the Lord in a burning bush (Exod. 3); Saul met God on the road to Damascus (Acts 9); and the apostles had the privilege of seeing Christ in the flesh for many years. The initial meeting was always followed up by constant communion. The same must apply to us; we must, on a regular basis, come into the presence of God, particularly if we are to lead others into His presence.

In ministering to people, there is a principle which must be acknowledged and adhered to, or ineffectiveness will inevitably follow. It is the truth expressed in Psalm 42:7, "Deep calls to deep at the sound of Thy waterfalls." We are only able to minister to the depth that we ourselves have plunged. There is a mysterious yet immutable correlation between what we know and what we are able to teach others, and where we have been and where we are able to take others. In communicating to others we can communicate from our mind to theirs or from our spirit to their spirits. The direction is always strictly horizontal. A truth which is only established in our minds will not touch the spirit of those to whom we are ministering. For a message to bring life to the hearer, it must first be bred deep in the leader's spirit. We may preach, teach, or sing on the subject of faith, but if our understanding of faith is merely a mental, intellectual one, we can only communicate on that level. Our audience may leave with a better understanding of the principles of faith, but they will not leave with faith in their hearts. This principle also applies to worship. We will not be able to lead a group of people in worship if we have not experienced genuine worhsip. A few isolated saints may enter the gates because of their personal praise life, but the majority of the people will go no further than we have gone as leaders.

One of the great challenges involved in leading worship is to not draw attention to any human flesh. The Lord has emphatically stated, "I am the Lord, that is My name; I will not give My glory to another, nor My praise to graven images" (Isa. 42:8). I believe the pride of man's flesh and the glory of God are mutually exclusive. If a man stands to lead people in worship, or even to teach, preach, or testify in such a manner as to draw attention to himself, the Lord will remove His glory from the midst of the assembly. This is why it is often difficult for a celebrity, a star athlete, a movie star, or another well-known personality, to really minister effectively. The novelty of having such a guest in the pulpit is hard to overcome. People are so enamored with the person that it is hard to direct their attention to Christ. Personally, I am not concerned or impressed with a person's credentials in the flesh; my concerns are "Do they walk with God?" and "Do they come with a fresh touch from the throne?" Those should be the criteria for spiritual service. The most effective guest worship leaders I have seen were those who were more concerned that God knew them than that men knew them.

A worship leader's primary goal is to exalt Jesus. Great singing is of little value if Christ is not made manifest in that singing. There must be a reality of His presence brought through sincere praise. We do not need to defend Christ; we need to exalt Him. If Jesus is lifted up in our midst, He will do the rest. He will reveal His love for the lost, He will pour out compassion and mercy on the needy, He will convict men of sin, He will heal the sick. In the worship service, Christ must be preeminently exalted.

I once asked the Lord to teach me how to encourage, how to prompt people to praise. I was tired of standing before the congregation and watching apathy prevail among so many saints. Many would not even attempt to enter worship; it appeared that some even begrudged what was going on. I prayed, "Lord, what can I do to lead these people into praise? How can I inspire them to participate and to desire the joy of worship?" As usual, the Lord had the answer to that question already penned in His Holy Word. Second Corinthians 4:15 says, "that the grace which is spreading to more and more people may cause the giving

Leading People in Worship

of thanks to abound to the glory of God." Giving of thanks, that is, praise, will abound and be plentiful when people see the grace of God spreading to more and more people, and particularly to themselves! The same thing is implied in Luke 19:37, "the whole multitude of the disciples began to praise God joyfully with a loud voice for all the miracles which they had seen."

Ideally, we should praise God for *who He is* and not just for what He has done; but that is not where most people are walking. We should be able to just say, "Jesus," and everyone would enter into praise, but the majority of saints are just not at that point in their praise life. People usually need to hear and see the grace of God poured out on living humans. Yes, the Lord delivered Daniel from the lion's den, but has He delivered anyone here from a terrible situation? We read in God's Word that Jesus healed Jairus' daughter, but has He healed anyone in your family lately? When these testimonies of God's power are shared, praise will erupt. This simply means that when God's people gather together, time must be set aside for the sharing of testimonies. I have learned that this must be done in an orderly, controlled manner, but that we must allow for sharing such as this. It lets everyone know that God is alive and well, and active in the lives of His beloved.

God had given me another insight into leading worship: we must begin with people where they are, and not where we are or hope they are or want them to be. It is no different than in any other area of Christian maturity. We do not discuss dispensationalism with a new Christian; we talk about baptism, prayer, and being filled with the Spirit. Many people have years of traditionalism engrained in their minds; many are inhibited because they do not know who they are in Christ. Embarrassing or intimidating these folks will only cause more damage. If they are simply instructed to be free and to follow the leading of the Spirit, *He* will lead them into worship. However, a word of caution should be stated. Never let the backslider set the mood or the speed at which you lead people into praise. There will always be those who refuse to journey. If you wait on these folks and let them set the tempo, the Spirit will be quenched. Find out where most of the people are and lead them.

I once heard Judson Cornwall (any serious student of praise should purchase of all of his books on the subject) comment that man can lead praise but only God can lead worship. This is marvelous insight. It is possible to orchestrate the praise time of a service but when God begins to manifest himself in worship, the praise leader best step aside and relinquish his role. This does not mean that he must literally step down off the platform (though it is often a good idea) but rather there must be a legitimate abdication of his authority in the service. When God comes He may want to move through conviction, in which case there will be a confession and tears of sorrow. The Lord may want to issue some commissions and appointments or He may simply instruct the people to enjoy His presence.

A leader of praise and worship should never hesitate to confess that he does not know where the Lord is leading in a particular service. Such honesty breeds respect among the saints. I realize that such a statement would develop apprehension among some praise leaders because of fear that a service may get "out of hand."

Two items will eliminate such apprehension. First, a mutual trust developed among a group of worshipers will deter any fear that something out of order may occur.

Leading People in Worship

Second, if the leader lets it be known that he will actively stop any disorderly conduct, this will develop confidence among the majority and put a word of caution in the minority.

I praise God for calling me to be a worship leader. It gives me more joy than anything else in life. Chances are good that you too will be in a position to influence the praise life of others; it may be leading the music in Sunday School, or having family devotions at home. Whenever and wherever the opportunity occurs, rejoice in it and be glad!

35
The Tabernacle of David

There is a fresh revelation of New Testament praise life nestled right in the midst of the books of the minor prophets. The verse is found in Amos 9:11: "In that day I will raise up the fallen tabernacle of David, and will wall up its breaches; I will also raise up its ruins, and rebuild it as in the days of old."

The tabernacle of David? I had studied the tabernacle of Moses, and Solomon's Temple, but what is the tabernacle of David? To find the answer involves a fascinating study which gives us great insight and instruction regarding the desired characteristics of our praise life.

God has always desired to dwell among men. In this current dispensation, God dwells among His people by the presence of the Holy Spirit in our lives. "And because you are sons, God has sent forth the Spirit of His Son into our hearts, crying, 'Abba! Father!' " (Gal. 4:6). In the person of Christ Jesus, "The Word became flesh, and dwelt among us" (John 1:14). Prior to the incarnation, God dwelt among His people in the ark of the covenant. When Moses first received plans for its construction, God said, "Construct a sanctuary for me, that I may dwell among them" (Exod. 25:8). God's residence was within the Holy of Holies, at the ark of the covenant. In 1 Chronicles 17:5, God confirms that His presence was in the ark of the covenant: "For I have not dwelt in a house since the day that I brought up Israel to this day, but I have gone from tent to tent and from one dwelling place to another." The ark of the covenant was not a symbol of God's presence; it was the dwelling place of God's presence.

I encourage you to pause a moment and read 1 Samuel, chapters 4 through 7, before proceeding. This will refresh our memory as to how the ark was captured by the Philistines, how it became a curse to them and how it was restored to Israel and found its resting place at Kirjath-jearim in the home of Abinadab.

It is sad to know that the ark of the covenant, the very presence and power of God, was, for the most part, ignored by God's people for the next one hundred years. All through the remainder of Samuel's ministry (forty years), through the reign of Saul (forty years) and for the first twenty years of David's ministry, the ark is mentioned only once (1 Sam. 14:18), and even then Saul did not properly acknowledge its holy character and intent.

Finally, David, the man after God's own heart, began to realize that something was missing! He began to have a deep desire for the presence of the living God. He consulted with every leader in the kingdom and with the priests and Levites, and said to them, "let us bring back the ark of our God to us" (1 Chron. 13:3). Kirjath-jearim (where the ark rested) was only eight miles from Jerusalem. The Bible records that David assembled all Israel together to retrieve the ark of the covenant: It was an impressive entourage.

The Tabernacle of David

They began to transport the ark toward Jerusalem, using a new cart drawn by oxen. Along the way the oxen stumbled, the ark began to fall, and Uzza, who drove the cart, reached out to steady the ark. God instantly struck him down. David became angry with the Lord and even retorted, "How can I bring the ark of God home to me?" (v. 12). There is a vital lesson to be learned from this incident. Though David had the right motive, he had the wrong manner. He tried to do the right thing the wrong way. God had given strict instructions that the ark was to be carried with poles and only on the shoulders of the Levites. Even in the mist of our seeking His presence, while we are worshiping and praising Him, God will not tolerate disobedience and sin. Praise will never appease God's wrath toward sin.

After this incident, David returned to Jerusalem for three months during which time he prepared a tabernacle, or tent, within which the ark would reside. I believe it is significant that, in addition to acknowledging his sin regarding the transport of the ark, David prepared a place of honor for the presence of God. Have we prepared an honorable place for the living God?

The second crusade to retrieve the ark was quite an undertaking. David gathered together the sons of Aaron, all the singers and instrumentalists he could find, and the captains of thousands to lead the march from Jerusalem. The processional was marked with great celebration and joy: "Thus all Israel brought up the ark of the covenant of the Lord with shouting, and with sound of the horn, with trumpets, with loud-sounding cymbals, with harps and lyres" (1 Chron. 15:28).

The Bible records only one person who was not inspired

by all the rejoicing: Michal, David's wife. When David was dancing before the Lord as the ark entered Jerusalem, she watched him out her window and despised him in her heart. When David returned home, she rebuked him, saying, "How the king of Israel distinguished himself today! He uncovered himself today in the eyes of his servants' maids as one of the foolish ones shamelessly uncovers himself" (2 Sam. 6:20). The Lord's judgment on her was, "and Michal the daughter of Saul had no child to the day of her death" (v. 23).

Michal's main problem was that she was in rebellion to her husband. David had commanded that *all* Jerusalem go up to retrieve the ark. Michal stayed at home. If she had been involved in the praise instead of just an onlooker, she might have been dancing as well. When God's children began to enter true, uninhibited praise, the onlookers will inevitably raise a deriding voice. It may even come from within the family! If our praise is sincere, it will not intimidate us; we will reply as David did, "It was before the Lord . . . therefore I will celebrate before the Lord" (v. 21).

The Israelites placed the ark in its prepared tent on Mount Zion and began a great praise service (1 Chron. 16). At the conclusion of the service David appointed Asaph and his relatives to "minister before the ark continually, as every day's work required" (v. 37). The ark was set high on a hill where the entire city could see it and hear the continual praises. Incidentally, understanding the praise of the ark on Mount Zion will revolutionize your reading of the Psalms. For instance, read Psalms 2:6, 48:1-11, 50:2, 74:2, 134:1-3, and imagine David, Asaph and the sons of Korah penning these lyrics while standing before the ark on Mount Zion.

The Tabernacle of David

That is how the Tabernacle of David was established. Now, back to the prophecy in Amos 9:11 (also see Acts 15:16). God is in the process of rebuilding the tabernacle of David among His people. Praise God He did not say He would restore the tabernacle of Moses. Only a very few could enjoy the ministry of Moses' tabernacle and only the high priest, once a year, could enter the presence of God. Worship would be very ritualistic and traditional, the priest performing the same ceremony day after day. Worship in the tabernacle of Moses was very restrained and silent. There were no instruments or singing; the only sound heard was that of the bells on the bottom of the priest's robe.

What a contrast to the tabernacle of David! All of Jerusalem entered the joyful praise of God. There was no order of worship. It was spontaneous celebration. There was music, shouting, dancing and great liberty. The ark of the covenant was placed in a conspicuous place and worshiped continually.

This is the type of environment God wants to dwell in today. This is the atmosphere in which He will manifest His powers and glory. One may ask, "Where does God want to establish the Tabernacle of David?" He will do so in the heart of an individual, in the life of a family, or in a local body of believers. He will inhabit any praise that is performed in spirit and in truth. I remind you, the Father *seeks* those who will truly worship Him (John 4:23).

Will David's tabernacle be rebuilt in your heart? Will you commit your family to a posture of continuous, spontaneous, uninhibited praise? Will you pray that your church will commit itself to the rebuilding of David's tent of meeting? God will honor and fulfill the words of the prophet Amos—He is doing it today. May we have the joy of participation and blessing.

36
In the Year King Uzziah Died

Isaiah chapter six records a marvelous worship experience. Isaiah literally saw the Lord, lofty and exalted. He saw the host of angels praising Him around the throne, and was even allowed to hear their antiphonal cry, "Holy, Holy, Holy, is the Lord of hosts, the whole earth is full of His glory." Isaiah was given access to the very throne room of the universe, a privilege given only to one other man in the Bible—John the Revelator.

It is significant that Isaiah prefaced his vision, "In the year of King Uzziah's death, I saw the Lord . . ."

It often takes a crisis to bring about confrontation. As long as our mode of operation is in the norm, our perception of the unusual will be dim. Even spiritually, when our lives are plodding along as usual, we will seldom see the mighty hand of God. It often takes a jolt to our status quo before we will have a confrontation with God. The year King Uzziah died was such an event. It was a time of crisis which prompted Isaiah's vision of the Lord.

Uzziah was sixteen years old when he became king. He did right in the sight of the Lord and, as long as he sought the Lord, the Lord prospered him (2 Chron. 26). Uzziah was successful in battle, which gave much peace of mind to the inhabitants of Jerusalem; he completed many civic projects which produced a spirit of progressiveness throughout Judah; agriculture prospered under his rule; and the invention of elaborate war machines caused his fame to be spread afar. "But when he became strong, his heart was so proud that he acted corruptly, and he was unfaithful to the Lord his God" (v. 16). When Uzziah became proud he did the same thing we do when we become proud. We attempt to do the work of the Lord in our own strength. We attempt to accomplish that which only God can do. Uzziah entered the Temple to burn incense on the altar, a service only the consecrated priests could perform. Azariah, the chief priest, and eighty valiant priests entered the Temple and opposed Uzziah and rebuked him. Uzziah continued in his obstinance and the Lord immediately struck him with leprosy, which he carried with him to his grave.

However, Scripture indicates that the latter days of Uzziah saw him return to the fear of the Lord. A good king had turned bad but turned good again before he died.

Apprehension surrounded the death of a king. History had proven the unpredictableness of the ones who ruled Judah. Prior to Uzziah, Amaziah had ruled Judah and led the people to idolatry. He was murdered in a conspiracy because he had turned away from following the Lord. Preceding Amaziah was Joash, who was a righteous and upright king, but he followed Ahaziah whose wicked reign only lasted one year. Ahaziah's father was Jeroram who was an evil king. He killed his own six brothers in order to secure his kingship; he also led the people to play the harlot.

In the Year King Uzziah Died

Prior to Jehoram, Jehoshaphat sat on the throne. His reign was blessed by the Lord and he did right in God's sight. It appeared that: as the king goes, so goes the country.

Judah had been plagued by inconsistent leadership, ruled sometimes by a good king, sometimes by a bad king. And it was not always "like father, like son"; often a godly king would be followed by his ungodly son. So the year King Uzziah died was a time of unrest and tenseness. Who would assume the kingship? Would he follow in the ways of Uzziah or would he oppress the people? During the transition would the Philistines, Arabians and Meunites seek revenge on Judah?

It was in this milieu that Isaiah saw the Lord—in the midst of conflict Isaiah had his confrontation with the Lord. But when Isaiah was at his lowest, he was elevated to his highest. In the midst of Isaiah's discouragement and trepidation, God revealed himself to His prophet. I believe there is a pattern reflected in this incident; not necessarily a principle, but a recurring pattern. When our circumstances reflect no divine touch, when our emotions seem seared and unresponsive, and when the future appears unsettled at best—God appears.

This was the experience of Job, a man God described as "blameless, upright, fearing God, and turning away from evil" (Job 1:1). He no doubt had sweet fellowship with God and enjoyed the holy presence. However, only after he suffered severely did he see the Lord clearly. In the final chapter of his saga, Job said, "I have heard of Thee by the hearing of the ear; but now my eye sees Thee; therefore I retract, and I repent in dust and ashes" (Job 42:5-6).

This was the experience of John the Revelator. John had walked with the Lord for three years. He enjoyed intimate times of friendship, teaching and communion. Yet it was while John was in exile on the isle of Patmos that he really saw the Lord. It happened on the Lord's day when he was in the Spirit; he saw Jesus as he had never seen Him before. No doubt John praised God for his exile experience.

Shadrach, Meshach, and Abednego, while in the midst of the fiery furnace, were visited by one who appeared "like the son of the gods." In the midst of conflict, they saw the Lord.

Is this not the pattern in our lives? The best times of worship have come in the midst of turmoil There are several reasons for this. Just as the two positive poles of a magnet repel each other, so pride and self-esteem repel us from the presence of God. The Lord says, "But to this one I will look, to him who is humble and contrite of spirit, and who trembles at My word" (Isa. 66:2). It often takes calamity to make us contrite. Furthermore, God sometimes orchestrates a removal from our lives of everything in which we trust, in order to show himself as the all-sufficient one. Again Isaiah said, "Woe to those who go down to Egypt for help, and rely on horses, and trust in chariots because they are many, and in horsemen because they are very strong, but they do not look to the Holy One of Israel, nor seek, the Lord" (Isa. 31:1). As long as we are looking to other things, we will probably not see the Lord.

There is yet another reason why this pattern of conflict and confrontation exists. Often trials enter our lives for the testing of our faith, to produce endurance, which makes us perfect and complete (James 1:2-4). God frequently rewards our successful completion of a trial by allowing us to enjoy His presence. There is nothing more encouraging to a spiritual-minded person than to have a fresh revelation of God.

What is the lesson to be learned? Perhaps only that the Lord is good and that He sometimes refreshes us after a storm. It would certainly be wrong to imply that the Lord is obligated to meet with us during these times. It is significant that Moses, when he saw the burning bush, said, "I must turn aside now, and see this marvelous sight, why the bush is not burned up" (Exod. 3:3). The Bible then records that "when the Lord saw that he turned aside to look, God called to him . . ." (v. 4). Had Moses not turned aside he would have missed a divine appointment with God.

One thing is for sure—five minutes in the presence of God is more than adequate compensation for years of crisis. Concerns of this world become insigificant in the light of His glory. Isaiah might have been concerned that the king was dead, but when he saw that the King of kings was alive and reigning, his heart was satisfied.

37
Upon Leaving His Presence

The ultimate goal of worship is to see God. If we do not come in touch with the living God, we have not worshiped. We may go through ritual, but if we do not enter the flow of His life, we have accomplished no more than mechanical exercise. But how marvelous it is when we enter true worship. Quite frankly, I live in anxious anticipation from one worship experience to the next. It is the zenith of life! True worship is heaven on earth.

But what happens after worship? When we leave (so to speak) the presence of God, or at least, leave the place of corporate or individual worship, what can we expect? Is praise and worship a panacea for all our ills? When we meet with God in worship, can we expect all our trying circumstances to dissipate? Should we expect all our friends and family to lose their fleshly tendencies? Should we take for granted that Satan and all his demons are forever rendered powerless? My experience has proven just the opposite. I have come to realize that after I have been in the presence of God, I can generally expect an attack on my life. It may be Satan attempting to regain lost ground, it may be my own fleshly nature revolting against the divine touch, it may be close friends or family who try my faith and the validity of my time spent with God. It may come in many different ways, through any number of people, but it will come.

This was the experience of Jesus in the later days of His life. Matthew twenty-six records the Lord's last supper with His disciples. The Lord knew of His impending death and announced that He would be betrayed by one of the twelve. He then administered the bread and the wine, sharing with them the mysterious symbolism it represented: "Take, eat; this is my body" and "Drink from it, all of you; for this is My blood of the covenant, which is to be shed on behalf of many for forgiveness of sins" (Matt. 26:26-27).

They finished their meal together with a time of praise: "And after singing a hymn, they went out to the Mount of Olives" (v. 30). The Greek word translated hymns is *humneo*, which literally translates to celebrate God in song, to sing praises unto God. In our vernacular we would say they sang a chorus of praise. It was not an aged hymn out of a dusty humn book; it was a fresh, anointed praise chorus. Because of the unusual circumstances surrounding the event, it was no doubt sung with much conviction and fervor. They took the time to pause, look heavenward, and enter a time of praise and worship. We are not sure how long they devoted themselves to praise. It could have been an extended session or a brief climax to a time of close communion. It probably closely followed Jesus' intimate conversation with His Father (John 17).

But what happened after the time of praise? Did Judas repent of his evil heart? Did the angels of glory surround and protect the Messiah? No, after the time of praise came

Upon Leaving His Presence

Gethsemane, the betrayal, Peter's denial, rejection by friends, and finally the cross.

As Jesus left the time of praise, He entered the trial of Gethsemane. There His heart was in such consternation in coming to grips with the Father's will that He sweat drops of blood. This was not the first time sweet communion was followed by trying times. Matthew three ends with the account of the baptism of Jesus. The Spirit of God descended upon Him as a dove and the voice of the Father was heard saying, "This is My beloved Son, in whom I am well-pleased" (v. 17). The next verse states, "Then Jesus was led up by the Spirit into the wilderness to be tempted by the devil" (Matt. 4:1). He was moved by the Spirit from fellowship with the Father to confrontation with the devil. We should not be alarmed when our journey takes a similar turn. We often think our time alone with God builds a hedge around us. We cannot imagine that God would lead us into various trials following such intimate fellowship. In reality, the times of worship prepare us for such trials. Had Jesus not been in the glorious presence of the Father in the praise service, He might have had difficulty deferring to the Father's will in the garden. But having seen the sovereign God in worship, Jesus was able to say, "Not my will but Thine be done." Had Jesus not experienced the outpouring of the Holy Spirit and heard His Father's audible voice while in the Jordan, the temptations of Satan in the wilderness might have been unbearable. Could it be that God, as He sees upcoming trials in our lives, graciously provides us with times of worship to strengthen our faith and reaffirm godly perspectives?

Not only did the circumstances take a drastic change for the worse, but, after the praise service, the Lord's closest friends had some very unspiritual reactions. Peter, James and John left the praise service, no doubt filled with ecstasy and a new love for Jesus and the Father; yet, within a short time they could not watch and pray with the Lord for one hour. Their keen insight was dimmed to the degree that they were unable to see the great need of the Lord. Later that same evening Peter experienced the lowest point in his life when he denied three times that he even knew the Lord. The same Jesus to whom he had vowed absolute loyalty during the praise service he had now treacherously denounced.

Often we feel that a deep experience of worship will make us invulnerable to acts of spiritual immaturity. Let us beware! Likewise, we expect our friends to support our spiritual plateau, most certainly not to test us and function as catalyst for demise. But praise is not a cure-all for our carnal nature. It is profitable to bring us to Jesus but it does not insure a final crucifixion of the Adamic nature.

Am I implying that praise has no effect on external circumstances or influence on others? Of course not. If this were my conviction I would have to remove many chapters of this book. Praise will change circumstances and particularly your perspective on circumstances. It can and will execute vengeance on Satan and his evil workers. Praise works! The point of balance to be achieved is simply that the ecstasy and glory arrived at during praise and worship are usually soon tempered by the reality of this evil and perverse world. Should this discourage us from seeking the Lord? Quite the opposite. If we do not regularly enjoy His presence and dine at His table, we will be powerless in the battle. The times of praise prepare us for the times of struggle. David "strengthened himself in the Lord" (1 Sam. 30:6) before he dealt with insurrection among his men and warfare with the Amalekites. Worship allows us to see God so that in the midst of adversity we retain hope.

For a man to drown, his head must be submerged. As long as our head is above water, the body can survive. Christ is the head, we are His body. Regardless of the insurmountable difficulties we may encounter, we rest assured that our head is seated in heaven. Though the body is submerged in trials, Christ our head is seated in glory. We know this blessed truth as a part of our doctrine but happy are we when, as Isaiah, we see the Lord high and lifted up. Then our difficulties, whether they be prior to or after the worship experience, will be met by one who has the blessed assurance.

38
Becoming Uninhibited

I am, by nature, a very unemotional and unexpressive person. On the one hand, this has proven a great asset through the years because it lends itself toward great stability—the low times are never very low and likewise the times of great celebration are also tempered. I never get depressed and I seldom get enthusiastically excited. The negative aspect of having such a temperament is that I have always had difficulty relating to people on an emotional level. It has been, and probably always will be, a challenge for me to be sensitive to the emotional needs of my wife and two daughters. The Lord knew I needed a house full of women, and to express my deep love for them on a consistent basis.

Another area my stoicism has adversely affected is my praise life, which involves the ability to express my love and affection to God. Just as I have had difficulty in expressing love to others, I had been lacking in my expressions to God. During the last five years, I have taken conscientious strides toward breaking through this barrier. Though not nearly as far along as I hope someday to be,

I feel at last that I can express my love to God at any time and in any way that will please Him, while I am alone or when in a group of people.

As I observe congregations across America, I sense that this is a common problem among our churches. Many people are not free to express themselves to God. Even those who are extroverted and generally verbose in nature become silent when it comes to praising God. Our society teaches us to be cautious and conservative; we build up facades to prohibit people from seeing who we really are. I wonder if it is possible to be transparent toward God if we cannot be transparent to one another.

To illustrate this dilemma, let me share an incident that happened several years ago during a revival meeting in Austin, Texas. I was not present at the meeting but I received a first-hand report. During the song service, a member of the congregation gently raised his hands as an offering of praise to God. As soon as the visiting evangelist came to the podium he said something like, "If you raise your hands, you better make sure you are doing so from a pure heart or God considers it sin." Well, the general idea of what he said is true; that is, any spiritual act done to be seen by men is sin (Matt. 6). But the way he said it and the untimeliness of the comment obviously put a damper on any further expressions. Later on in the service, about halfway through the sermon, a light-hearted reference was made to the University of Texas football team. The pianist stealthily made his way to the piano and began playing the U.T. fight song, at which time the majority of the congregation rose to their feet and raised both arms in the air, giving the "hook-em-horns" sign with their hands. What a marvelous, spontaneous outburst of emotion.

Becoming Uninhibited

Unfortunately it was directed toward the U.T. football team and not toward God. Why is it that in so many areas of life we can be very outward but in our relating to God we are bound to a less exciting norm?

I believe the root of this problem is expressed in John 12:42-43. The Bible states: "Nevertheless many even of the rulers believed in Him, but because of the Pharisees they were not confessing Him, lest they should be put out of the synagogue; for they loved the approval of men rather than the approval of God." Beloved, we must confess to God that deep in our hearts we are men-pleasers and not God-pleasers. As long as we are seeking the approval of men, we will not find the approving nod of our heavenly Father. The two are mutually exclusive. Jesus spoke of it when He said, "No one can serve two masters; for either he will hate the one and love the other, or he will hold to one and despise the other. You cannot serve God and mammon" (Matt. 6:24).

I can recall specific times in my life when God had to deal severely with my man-consciousness. Once I was studying in the main academic library at North Texas State University in Denton, Texas. With as much clarity as an audible voice, God told me to walk out into the main foyer, get down on my knees, and pray. I obeyed, though reluctant at first. With every passing moment there was a tearing down of the flesh, a crucifying of the desire for the approval of man.

In a similar incident, I was leading music during a conference at my church when, during the invitation, the Lord told me to bow low before Him (the Hebrew *shaha* translated "to worship" literally means to "bow low"). I immediately went to my knees only to sense that the Lord was telling me to bow lower. I then bent over and put my elbows on the floor, but the Spirit was still not satisfied. I finally stretched out on the floor on my face, and lay prostrate. Truthfully, thoughts were racing through my mind such as, "What are people going to think?" but soon I reached a peaceful state in which it really did not matter what people thought because I was being obedient and pleasing to God. It often takes specific acts such as these to develop in our lives an ability to uninhibitedly express ourselves to God. For some it may be the raising of hands, for another it may mean praying aloud in a Sunday school class, or singing a solo, or shouting to God. The key is to obey the Spirit of God as He leads us out of bondage and into the freedom of free expression.

In addition to these times of personal teaching, the Lord, through the testimony of several individuals in the Bible, has encouraged my heart toward being expressive to Him.

The story of David bringing the ark of the covenant into Jerusalem has always been an inspiration to me. In the midst of the processional he danced before the Lord with all his might. There was a lot of shouting and singing accompanying the march, and David even removed his kingly robes (he did wear a linen ephod the entire time). Can you imagine King David, the mighty warrior, the potentate of Israel, behaving in such a manner? Surely the king would be more dignified, surely he would view the triumphal entry but not participate in such extremes! To the contrary, David's heart was full of the praise of God and he was not ashamed to demonstrate to God and to his people his joy in the Lord. Incidentally, I am sure that as a leader David's spontaneous expressions gave his people great freedom in their actions. In like manner, the pastor must be the ultimate praise leader in the church. His people will not feel entirely comfortable going beyond the leadership of their pastor. David should be an inspiration to all of us. His total abandonment to God is refreshing and should encourage us toward boldness in the Lord.

Mary, the mother of Jesus, is another example of one who cared more for the approval of God than the approval of men. Do we realize what she went through during her pregnancy and probably what she continually faced for the rest of her life? As a young Jewish virgin, she conceived in her womb the Messiah by the Holy Spirit. She suddenly had to answer some very difficult questions. She had to share with Joseph, with whom she was engaged, the fact that she was pregnant. Her parents could not imagine what had happened. When interrogated about the source of her pregnancy she would reply that she was expecting from the hand of God. Less understanding were her neighbors; no doubt it was the talk of the town. Not only was Mary expecting a child but she said that God was responsible. Perhaps only Joseph and a few close friends and relatives really believed her. The others probably considered her immoral and a liar.

What would prompt Mary to bear these false accusations for her entire life? Mary was a God-pleaser and not a man-pleaser. She had heard Gabriel deliver the message of God: "Hail, favored one! The Lord is with you . . . Do not be afraid, Mary: for you have found favor with God" (Luke 1:28, 30). The favor of God was more important to her than the favor of man. Such should be the testimony of our lives.

Sometime ago, the Lord opened my eyes to yet another biblical example of one who was committed to being a God-pleaser. When the Holy Spirit spoke to my heart, it was like a cap-stone was put on this issue—it was now settled in my heart. I should have known all along that Jesus is the prime and ultimate example of all spiritual truths. As we look to Him, we see truth personified. The specific revelation had to do with the death of Jesus. I was taken back to that tragic day that the Lord God was hung between two thieves and treated like an abased criminal. I was made to see that down through the ages, in all portraits and all sculptures portraying the crucifixion, the artist, out of reverence to Christ, had portrayed the suffering Messiah as having worn a loin cloth. In reality, the Lord hung naked on the cross. The most modest man in all the world was made to hang naked before the world. Perhaps it was at this moment that He was tempted to cry out, "Father, this is enough, I will not bear the shame of the cross!" But He did not. The writer of Hebrews says that Jesus, "for the joy set before Him, endured the cross, despising the shame" (Heb. 12:2). Christ went through the agony and the shame of the cross because He was intent on pleasing the Father. Beloved, if the Holy Son of God went to such great lengths to pursue obedience to God and to maintain His Father's approval, at what point should we stop? At what point in our lives should we resist and say, "I will no longer tolerate this, you are asking too much of me"? Can we dare say to God, "My praise of you must be tempered by what is traditional or what is accepted by all"?

I hope I deserve the following words on my epitaph: "Here lie the mortal remains of Don McMinn—he was a fool for Christ's sake." Paul was considered such many times (Acts 17:18, 26:24) because "the cross is to those who are perishing foolishness, but to those who are being saved it is the power of God" (1 Cor. 1:18).

Am I advocating ludicrous actions or embarrassing scenes? Certainly not. I am encouraging us all to live in the freedom Christ has provided for us. Particularly in our praise life, we should be free to express our love and affection to God in any way He leads us and not be intimidated by any source that does not have the mark of God upon it. Regardless of what man may say, we must be solely given to the ultimate directive of the universe—the praise and worship of God.

Selected Bibliography

Allen, Ronald Barclay, *Praise—A Matter of Life and Breath* (Nashville, TN, 1980: Nelson).

Allen, Ronald and Gordon Borror, *Worship—Rediscovering the Missing Jewel* (Portland, OR, 1982: Multnomah Press).

Baker, E. Charlotte, *On Eagle's Wings* (Seattle, WA, 1979: The King's Temple).

Cornwall, Judson, *Let Us Praise* (South Plainfield, NJ, 1973: Bridge), *Let Us Worship* (South Plainfield, NJ, 1983: Bridge).

Murchison, Anne, *Praise and Worship In Earth as it is in Heaven,* (Waco, TX, 1981: Word Books).

Taylor, Jack, *The Hallelujah Factor* (Nashville, TN, 1984: Broadman).

Tozer, A.W. *Worship—The Missing Jewel of the Evangelical Church* (Harrisburg, PA, 1961: Christian Pub).

Westermann, Claus, *Praise and Lament in the Psalms* (Atlanta, GA, 1981: John Knox Press).